The Mystery and Magic of Trees and Flowers

LESLEY GORDON

Grange
BOOKS

ACKNOWLEDGEMENTS

PICTURE CREDITS
The publishers would like to thank the following for supplying
illustrations:

Colour
Baxter Print (E. T. Archive) 10 above; Bodleian Library 15 below, (E. T.
Archive) 82 below; British Library 11, 47 above, 63 above; British
Museum 10 below, (E. T. Archive) 22 below, (E. T. Archive) 99 above;
City of Manchester Art Galleries (E. T. Archive) 98 above E. T. Archive
59 below, 63 below, 82 above, Fine Art Photographic Library frontis-
piece 30 above, 54 above left , 54 above right; Leipzig Museum (Robert
Harding Associates) 83; National Gallery (E. T. Archive) 15 above;
Novosti Press Agency 47 below; Uffizi, Florence (Scala) 39 below;
Sothebys (E. T. Archive) 59 above; Städelsches Kunstinstitut 22 above;
Tate Gallery (E. T. Archive) 98 below.

Black and white
British Library 49 left, 49 right; British Museum (E. T. Archive) 81;
E. T. Archive 26, 37, 64, 88, 89; Fine Art Society 67, 69; National
Gallery (E. T. Archive) 16, 18; Victoria and Albert Museum 21.

First published in Great Britain 1985 by
Webb & Bower (Publishers) Limited

Copyright © Webb & Bower (Publishers) Limited 1985

This edition published 1993 by Grange Books
An imprint of Grange Books Limited
The Grange
Grange Yard
London
SE1 3AG

Produced by The Promotional Reprint Company Ltd. UK

ISBN 1 85627 495 0

Printed and bound in China

Contents

Introduction

People with green fingers often admit, with an apologetic smile, that they talk to their flowers – a little encouragement to a tired-looking pot-plant perhaps, or a few words of congratulation to something small in the herbaceous border.

Seldom, however, does anyone listen to plants. We do not hear, or do not want to hear, the protests of a right-handed honeysuckle tied to a trellis by a left-handed gardener. We close our ears to the cries of pain and protest of a contented weed ruthlessly torn from its birthplace and condemned to die on the compost heap.

That communication once took place between plants and men seems certain. Olympus and the green world were closely interwoven, until Olympus was no more, and the green world continued alone in the rhythm of its seasons. In folklore, strange properties were given to plants without apparent reason, and accepted without question. Fern seed was known to render men invisible; cowslips could open locks, and a mandrake screamed when it was dug up. All this plant lore was widely believed, indicating that some understanding, or at times misunderstanding, was taking place between man and plant. Why should the orpine have been regarded as so reliable a divination plant 200 years before Francis Kilvert wrote in his diary on 11 June 1873, 'In Gander Lane we saw in the banks some of the Midsummer Men plants which my mother remembers the servant maids and cottage girls sticking up in their houses and bedrooms on Midsummer Eve for the purpose of divining their sweethearts'? From what deep roots came the belief that the world was some kind of mystic fruit of the Universe Tree, and that man and woman were born of the Tree of Life? Why the symbolism of the lotus springing from the navel of Vishnu, and what caused flowers to rise from the blood of dead heroes?

From these mysterious beginnings evolved The Language of Flowers, which in more leisurely days seized the imagination of the young and romantic. Even Mark Twain, in the person of Tom Sawyer, understood the meaning of a pansy tossed over the garden fence by a pig-tailed siren in embroidered pantalettes. Looking in the opposite direction, Tom picked up the pansy between his dusty toes, and surreptitiously stuffed it inside his jacket next to his heart. 'A pansy for thoughts' gave Tom plenty to think about that day.

The leisure has gone, and perhaps the romance and the nonsense, but a rose offered by a man to a woman still brings the same message.

Honeysuckle climbing a honeysuckle stairway and feeding her pet goat with its favourite leaf, Caprifoly, caprifolium or goat leaf, the old names for honeysuckle.

Man and the tree

When man began to seek some explanation of his origins, and of the origin of the world in which he found himself, the descent of the human race from a tree became a widespread belief. The unfolding of leaves and the expanding of branches were taken as a symbol of life, and trees were made the object of veneration. In man's imagination trees began to be peopled with hamadryads and dryads, wood nymphs and fairies, demons and fawns, and to some even the world was believed to have been born of a vast tree, the greatest of all trees, the Universe Tree, the World Tree, or the Mundane Tree.

In the Norse Edda writings, a vast ash tree, Yggdrasil, represented the life-giving forces of nature, larger and more powerful than man. The World Tree acted as a sort of prop to the roof of the sky. It sprang from the subterranean source of all matter, and its widespread branches were the celestial regions, its leaves were the clouds, and its fruits the stars. The dew that dripped from the tree men called honey-dew, and it was the food of bees. There were three main stems to the Yggdrasil; the centre stem ran up through the Midgard, the earth, and issued out of the mountain Asgard, where the gods assembled at the base of Valhalla, reached only by Bifrost, the bridge of the rainbow. The second stem of Yggdrasil sprang up in Muspellsheim, where the Past, the Present and the Future dwelt, and the gods sat in judgement. The third stem rose in Nifleheim, the cold north, where all the knowledge of mankind flowed from the fountain of the Frost-giant, Mimir, the personification of Wisdom. One day the god Odin, who regulated the periods of day and night, and of the changing seasons, came and begged for a draught of water from this fountain, but he was obliged to leave one of his eyes in payment for it. This, it is believed, symbolized the descent of the sun every evening, the mead that was quaffed by Mimir each morning being the rosy dawn.

Believers in some sort of Universe Tree must already have been familiar with tree worship, and this idealizing process most probably gave birth to the closely related Tree of Knowledge, and the Tree of Life. It must be remembered that these names were applied to whatever species of tree flourished in each particular climate of the world, and that the most ancient types of Life Tree are the ash, the cedar, the date and the fig, and these are the trees that were most venerated.

The sacred tree of Buddha is the peepul (pipal) or bo tree, *Ficus religiosa*, native to Hindustan and Ceylon, and worshipped by the Buddhists of India. It is the Tree of Knowledge under which Buddha sat, with the resolve that he would not rise until he had attained the knowledge that 'maketh free'. It is the cloud tree where the heavenly flame is stored, guarded by dark demons. It is also the Tree of Buddha, the Way of Safety, because it grew by the river that separates earth from heaven, and is the only way that mortals may pass from the shores of this world to those of the unseen world beyond.

Under the banyan, *Ficus indica*, a related sacred tree, it is said that Vishnu was born, the second of the triad of Brahma, Vishnu and Shiva. Vishnu was regarded as the preserver, while Brahma was the creator and Shiva the destroyer. In India each Buddha was associated with his own *bodhi*-tree, a fig tree that was also a tree of wisdom.

. The Indian Cosmic Tree was the symbol of vegetation, of universal life and of immortality; a combination of the Universe Tree and the Tree of Life. In the sacred Vedic writings, it was from this tree of many names that men first sustained and nourished life. As the Ambrosial tree, the tree yielding immortal food, it was known as Amrita or Soma,

The World Tree of the Iranians was the Haoma, the sacred
vine of the Zoroastrians, shown here growing up a tree
in this Persian manuscript painting of the sixteenth century.

OPPOSITE ABOVE:
Yggdrasil, the Mundane Tree or World Tree.
In the Norse Edda writings, Yggdrasil, a vast ash tree, represented the
life-giving forces of nature and acted as a prop to the roof of the sky.

OPPOSITE BELOW:
Indian ascetics seated under a banyan tree.
(Seventeenth-century Mughal painting.) It is said that
Vishnu was born under a banyan tree.

Asclepius acida. The soma is not only a plant, but also a powerful deity. The ambrosia of the gods was in essence identical with soma, but the Hindu Soma is supernaturally the god Brahma himself. The Indian sacred writings describe a cloud tree, which by its shadows produced day and night, before the creation of the sun and the moon. In the form of the soma, the World Tree becomes the Tree of Paradise, the king of all trees and vegetation, as well as the god Soma to be worshipped. Soma is sometimes concealed in clouds, sometimes in soft and silvery light as the great Indu, the moon. It is therefore characterized as the Moon-tree or Moon-plant. Out of this tree the immortals shaped heaven and earth.

The World Tree of the Iranians was the Haoma, the sacred vine of the Zoroastrians. It is both tree and god, and gives strength and health to the body, and to the soul enlightenment and eternal life. A life-giving drink was prepared from the terrestrial haoma, which was taken with prayer and with its own liturgy.

There is less evidence of the existence of tree worship among the Chinese, although they too have a tradition of a Tree of Life, and a drink of immortality made from various sacred plants. This Tree of Life was the cassia tree, native to Southern China, an evergreen with an aromatic bark, and bearing long cylindrical fragrant pods. Legend tells that this Tree of Life has grown from ages past to an incredible height in Paradise, a garden high up in the Tibetan mountains at the source of the Yellow River. Another ancient belief was that a cassia grew in the middle of the moon, which was then called the Disc of Cassia. The development of its flower was equated with the phases of the moon.

Japanese mythology tells of the holy *sakaki* trees growing on the Mountain of Heaven, and of a herb of immortality to be gathered on the Island of Eternal Youth. This island has the traditional characteristics of the earthly paradise, endless spring, unclouded skies, unfading flowers, and birds forever

singing with love and joy. Sorrow, pain and death are unknown. This Japanese legend preserves the connection between Paradise and the Cosmic Tree, and each nation, according to its culture, emphasized one aspect of it. The intellectual Buddhist saw in it the emblem of knowledge; the Persian regarded it as the Tree of Immortality, and the Hebrews, occupied with the idea of man's frailty, made it the Tree of Temptation. Certain old trees growing near Shinto temples are regarded as sacred, and there is a legend of an enormous metal pine that grew in the north, at the centre of the world.

The belief of the Greeks and Romans, that the human race was the fruit of the ash, was also common among the Teutons. Hesiod relates that it was from the trunks of ash trees that Zeus created the third or bronze race of men. The ash was thought of by the Greeks as an image of the clouds, and the nymphs of the ash were a race of cloud goddesses; they adopted the oak trees as the first mothers of men. Virgil wrote that:

> These woods were first the seat of sylvan powers,
> Of nymphs and fawns, and savage men who took
> Their birth from trunks of trees and stubborn oak.

Ovid tells us that the simple food of the primitive race consisted largely of 'Acorns dropping from the tree of Jove'.

At Dodona, an ancient town in Epirus, perhaps the oldest of the Greek sanctuaries, Zeus was worshipped in his sacred oak, *Quercus*. Here in a grove of oaks, an oracle tree, the oak of the god himself, was consulted, and his responses were interpreted from the rustling of its branches, the murmur of the sacred spring which rose at its foot, or from the drawing of the oracle lots kept in an urn beneath it. The virtue of this oracular oak was not only transmitted to its offshoots, but even preserved in the dead wood after its separation from the tree. A beam hewn from the Dodona oak was built into Jason's *Argo* as a talisman, which constantly gave the Argonauts advice and warning. In ancient Rome, Jupiter was originally worshipped in the form of a lofty oak tree which grew upon the Capitol, and was later identified with the Greek Zeus.

There are many instances in classical mythology where flowers were believed to have arisen from the life-blood of a slain god. Of less violent origin were the flowers who grew from the tear drops of sad lovers. These legends of the flower gods and goddesses were based on Mount Olympus in Thessaly, where at the gate of clouds kept by the goddesses of the Seasons the passage of the celestials to earth took place, and where they were admitted on their return.

The Father of the Sun, Moon and Dawn was Hyperion. He is therefore the original sun-god, and is painted with the splendour and beauty which was afterwards bestowed on Apollo. To Apollo, as the sun-god, the cornel, *Cornus mas*, tree was offered, and a festival in his honour, known as the Cornus, was held as an appeasement because the Greeks had cut down a consecrated thicket of cornus trees on Mount Ida. Apollo fell in love with Hyacinthus, son of Amyclas, King of Sparta, which aroused the jealousy of Zephyr, the West wind. One day, when Apollo and Hyacinthus were playing at quoits on the banks of the Eurotas, Zephyr, in his jealous rage, turned aside the quoit that the sun-god had thrown, so that it struck Hyacinthus and killed him. Keats alludes to this legend in *Endymion*, where he describes the lookers-on at the tragedy:

> Or they might watch the quoit-pitchers, intent
> On either side, pitying the sad death
> Of Hyacinthus, when the cruel breath
> Of Zephyr slew him –

OPPOSITE BELOW:
Phaeton, with his father Helios (the Sun). Rashly claiming his ability to drive his father's chariot across the skies in its daily journey from east to west, Phaeton was unable to control the horses and fell headlong from the heavens, his hair ablaze, into the great river Eridanus. His lamenting sisters were turned into black poplar trees on the banks of the river, and their tears became amber as they dropped into the stream.

Adonis, the favourite of Venus, who was killed while hunting wild boar. At the request of Venus, the adonis flower sprang from the drops of his blood.

The Greek legend of Apollo and Daphne tells how Apollo was
consumed with unrequited love for Daphne, who escaped him by
turning into a laurel tree at the moment of capture. Apollo then chose
the laurel for his sacred tree.

It was from the blood of Hyacinthus that arose the
flower that has since borne his name.

Another story of Apollo is concerned with his
love for Daphne. The legend tells how, after a quarrel
with Apollo, Cupid shot him with a golden arrow,
and then shot Daphne with an arrow of lead.
Immediately Apollo was consumed with love for
Daphne, while she abhorred the thought of loving.
Daphne fled, but with little chance of escape. With
failing strength she prayed to the gods for help, and
with Apollo's outstretched arms about to seize her,
the gods took pity, and she was turned into a laurel,
Laurus, tree. Apollo's love proved constant, and he
chose the laurel for his sacred tree, and wore a wreath
of its scented leaves in memory of Daphne.

Clytie was a water-nymph, daughter of Oceanus
and Tethys. She fell in love with Apollo, who did not

return her passion. The sad Clytie pined away, sitting on the cold ground, her golden hair uncombed, tasting neither food nor drink, and gazing on the sun as he rose and as he set, her eyes fixed constantly on him. At last her limbs rooted in the earth and her face became a flower, the sunflower, which was made the emblem of Constancy. A fate that was better than she deserved.

The adonis flower, *Flos adonis*, owes its name and some say its very existence, to the favourite of Venus, Adonis, who was killed while hunting wild boar. At the request of Venus, the scarlet adonis flower arose from the life-blood of the dying boy. At Byblos, the local belief was that the river turned red with this blood every year, when the rains came and washed the coloured earth into the river. There was an annual feast of Adonis held at Byblos, Alexandria and Athens, for which were planted jars of fennel, dill and lettuce, which were called Adonis gardens. The morning after the festival they were thrown away, and thus short-lived perishable things became known as Adonis gardens.

When Phaeton, the son of Helios and Clymene, drove his father's chariot across the skies, unable to control the horses, he fell headlong from the heavens, his hair ablaze, and the great river Eridanus received his burning body. The naiads raised a tomb for him inscribed with these words:

> Driver of Helios' chariot, Phaeton
> Struck by Jove's thunder, rests beneath this stone,
> He could not rule his father's car of fire,
> Yet it was much nobly to aspire.

His sisters, the Heliades, lamenting his fate, were turned to black poplar trees, *Populus nigra*, on the banks of the river, and their tears became amber as they dropped into the stream.

Admetus was a suitor for the hand of Alcestis, the daughter of Pelias, who had promised her to one who should come for her in a chariot drawn by lions and boars. This task Admetus performed, and he was rewarded with the possession of the beautiful Alcestis. But Admetus fell ill and was near to death, until Apollo prevailed upon the Fates to spare him. This they did, on condition that he found someone who would consent to die in his stead. Alcestis sacrificed her own life to save her husband, and for her great goodness she was restored to the world in the form of a daisy. A small flower to acknowledge so great a debt.

Possibly the best known of all flower legends is that of Narcissus, son of Cephisus and Liriope. Narcissus, denying the love of man or woman, worshipped his own beautiful image, reflected in a pool. Trying to reach his shadow he fell into the water and was drowned. Echo, a nymph who had loved Narcissus in vain, came weeping with her sister nymphs to remove his body, but it had disappeared. Only a white flower floated on the water, but we can still hear Echo calling in the emptiness of deserted

The young Narcissus, seeing himself for the first time, reflected in the pool under the rocks of Mount Helicon. Painted by Giovanni Antonio Boltraffio (1467–1516), a pupil of Leonardo da Vinci.

places. A sad story, but as Emilia said to her servant in *The Two Noble Kinsmen*,

That was a fair boy certaine, but a foole
To love himselfe; were there not maids enough?

When Orpheus was grieving for the loss of his wife Eurydice, shut away from him forever in the darkness of the Underworld, he was torn to pieces by the Thracian women who resented his indifference to their overtures. His head was thrown into the River Hebros, down which it rolled into the sea, and was borne across to Lesbos. Where his lyre fell there bloomed the first violet, the embodiment of pure music. The astronomers taught that the lyre was taken by Zeus and placed among the stars, and ever since the violet has been dedicated to Orpheus.

The ancient allegory of the Seasons tells how Persephone (Proserpine) was captured and borne off to the Underworld by Dis (Pluto). Her inconsolable mother, Demeter (Ceres), sought for her child throughout the length and breadth of Sicily. At last, sad and weary, she sat down upon a stone, and there remained for nine days and nights. The gods caused poppies to spring up round her feet and Demeter stooped, breathing their bitter scent and tasting their seeds, until she forgot her sorrow in the oblivion of sleep. Finally Persephone was restored to her mother, but this is a story without an end, for Persephone is the seed corn concealed in the earth, reappearing with the spring, and then disappearing once more with the coming of winter. She is sought for by Demeter, goddess of the harvest and the bringer of agriculture to the world. The poppies are the emblem of sleep, and when bread is decorated with poppy seeds or grain, we may remember the story of Persephone and Demeter, and the cycle of agricultural life.

Paradise and the sacred plants

Paradise, or the Garden of Delight, is to be found in nearly all the nations of antiquity. The tradition varies, and Paradise may be found represented as the seat of the gods, the first garden of the parents of mankind, or the abode of the spirits of the blessed. The home of the gods was assumed to be the marvellous tree whose branches were the sky, and its fruits the sun and stars, or the mountain whose summit touched and supported the heavens. The second belief, that the first parents were born from trees, led to the idea that these honoured ancestors lived among trees in an ideal garden, to Christians the Garden of Eden. The third concept grew when there arose the belief in a future life of reward or punishment, a heaven and hell.

The first of these mythological gardens is best found in the literature of India, where in the Garden of Indra the gods took their ease, among miraculous trees, luminous flowers and fruits that conferred immortality, and where the sweetest music accompanied the music of the birds.

The second concept, of our first parents and the serpent, may be seen in sacred books and the carvings on ancient seals and cylinders, as belonging to the beliefs of many different races. John Gerard (1545–1612), surgeon, botanist and author of the famous *Herbal* (1597), wrote of these Gardens of Delight:

> Talke of perfect hapinesse or pleasure, and what place was so fit for that, as the garden place, wherein Adam was set, to be the Herbarist? Whither did the poets hunt for their syncere delights, but into the gardens of Alcinous, of Adonis, and the orchards of the Hesperides?

The third conception, of paradise as the dwelling of the righteous dead, can be found in the earliest Greek literature and in the Koran, the sacred book of Islam. The Jewish Talmud has an upper paradise and a lower paradise, and between them is fixed a pillar by which they are joined together, and which is called 'The strength of the Hill of Sion', a survival of the World Tree.

Paradise, it seems, is a factual as well as a spiritual reproduction of a better, more peaceful and more beautiful world than that in which the believer finds himself, and in a map of the thirteenth century it may be seen, firmly located as a circular island to the east of India. The cartographer has even marked the gate from which our first parents were expelled.

The sacred meanings given to plants have been handed down from generation to generation, through religions and through nations, and one plant may have acquired many names or, the reverse, a single name may have been adopted for many plants. So highly venerated is the lotus (lotos) that it appears as a symbolic ornament in architecture and sculpture, in the capitals of columns, in wall paintings and friezes and ancient papyri, and held in the

Vishnu, the Preserver in Hindu theology, on the serpent of eternity. From his navel springs a lotus plant, in the calyx of which Brahma is seated, ready to accomplish the work of creation.

The Garden of Paradise, from a German painting of the fifteenth century.

A thirteenth-century 'World Map', the so-called 'Psalter' map, showing Paradise located at the top of the circle.

crossed arms of Egyptian mummies. The Egyptians cultivated three species, the *Nymphae cerulea*, or blue-flowered lotus; the *Nymphae lotus*, a white flowered variety and the *Nelumbium speciosum* or sacred bean, with brilliant red flowers.

The lotus in its various colours and forms was sacred to the Greeks as a symbol of beauty and eloquence. In Hindu theology a golden lotus brought forth the god Brahma. Vishnu, the preserver, is represented with four arms, and from his navel springs a lotus plant, in the calyx of which Brahma is seated, ready to accomplish the work of creation. It is used as a symbol of a Buddha in both India and China, and as the emblem of paradise in Japan. Four thousand years ago it was known as the sacred bean of Egypt and the rose-lily of the Nile. In different form and colours the lotus represents the sacred aspirations of a wide area of the world.

The cultivated olive, *Olea europaea*, has an ancient history, rooted in the dark beginning of the wild olive. It is believed that it has been in cultivation for at least 5000 years. The earliest known olive groves existed in Egypt, and in the southern part of Crete. Archaelogical finds have established that olive culture played an important part in these two early civilizations. In the palace at Knossos there was a Room of the Olive Press, and the great jars in which the oil was stored may still be seen. The virtues of the god-given tree, the providing of a better and more varied diet as well as the introduction of lamp-oil, which brought primitive peoples from darkness into light, have made the olive the most valued and most frequently mentioned tree both in Roman classics and in Christian literature. 'And thou shalt command the children of Israel, that they bring thee pure oil olive beaten for the light, to cause the lamp to burn always' (Exodus 27: 20). Jesus spent his last night of freedom in the vicinity of an olive tree in the Garden of Gethsemane, whose name means 'the garden with the olive press'. To a large part of Christendom, anointment with olive oil has symbolism.

In a Greek legend, Athena, the goddess of Wisdom, and Poseidon, the god of the Mediterranean, could not decide which of them should name the newly founded city of Athens. The other gods decreed that whoever gave the most useful gift to the inhabitants of the earth should be allowed the privilege. Poseidon struck the earth with his trident and a horse appeared. Athena then struck the earth and an olive tree sprang up. The gods decided that the olive, as the emblem of peace, was the most valuable to mankind, so Athens was named after Athena, its protectress, and earth is still waiting for the gift of peace.

It seems that the reason the olive became and remains a worldwide symbol of peace is that, in its early cultivation, decades passed between the planting of the seed and the final harvest of the fruit, and no man who did not desire a long and peaceful life for himself, with a satisfying provision for posterity, would plant an olive grove. Its association with the gentle dove, according to a German tradition, begins with the tomb of Adam, from which sprang an olive tree. From this olive the leaf was plucked that the dove carried back to Noah: 'And the dove came in to him in the evening; and, lo, in her mouth was an olive leaf pluckt off: so Noah knew that the waters were abated from off the earth' (Genesis 8: 11).

The vine, *Vitis vinifera*, was probably the first of nature's gifts to be cultivated, sharing with the fig and the olive the symbolism of peace, and the prosperity that accompanies peace. Among the ancients, it was dedicated to Bacchus, and figures of this merry god were crowned with vine leaves and decorated with the vine's trailing stems and tendrils, and bunches of purple and golden grapes. Tradition points to Greece as its native country. More than sixty varieties were cultivated by the Greeks and Romans, and a considerable amount of instruction on the art of viniculture of the period remains. The elm was commonly used as a prop for vines, a practice that gave rise to numerous poems on the theme of 'the fair and straight-limbed elm' and 'the beauteous and marriageable Vine', whose marriage festival was held with great rejoicing. A fig was also used as a vine support, and the well-known biblical quotation from Micah (4: 4), 'they shall sit every man under his vine and under his fig tree; and none shall make them afraid', is believed to refer to this close association.

Since the origin of the vine is beyond human recollection, man has invented his own explanations in legends that are probably more satisfying than the truth. When Adam and Eve were in Paradise, God sent His Angel to drive them forth. The Angel grieved for them, and when he returned to Paradise he struck his staff into the ground and wept. The staff grew, and shortly became a tree. 'Then he gave of it to Adam and said to him, "Sow seed of this". And Adam did so, and the name of the tree is the Vine.'

Noah planted a vineyard when he stepped from the Ark on to dry land, and he is the first on record to have made wine, thereby starting one of the most important and profitable occupations in the world. The vine was one of the earliest symbols of the Redeemer, in His own words to the Apostles, 'I am the Vine, ye are the branches' (St John, 15: 5). Constantine the Great, the first Christian emperor of Rome, made the Vine a symbol of the Christian faith.

Although the vine has been honoured frequently in the Bible, the dark side of this gift of God has not been ignored; indeed, since Noah made wine, drunkenness has been condemned in the Old Testament and the New. Isaiah makes it clear: 'Woe unto them that rise up early in the morning, that they may follow strong drink; that continue until night, till wine inflame them!' (5: 11).

Although the grape-bearing vine is the Biblical vine that transcends all the other vines, cucumbers, melons and gourds are all mentioned, and there is also the symbolical Tree or Rod of Jesse. This was founded on no actual plant, but on medieval works

The Tree of Jesse, in a late thirteenth-century English psalter.

of imagination and art, based on the prophecy by the dying Jacob of the coming of a Messiah. Sculpted in stone at the back of an altar, forming the tracery of an abbey window, brilliant with rich colouring in glass, fresco or embroidery, the Tree of Jesse may still be seen. Many branched candelabra, once known as Jesse-trees, but later commonly called 'spiders', once shone in churches and homes. The recumbent figure of Jesse is represented with a vine rising from his loins, and may also be seen in stained-glass windows, known as Jesse-windows. The name inevitably settled on some suitable plant, and Vara di Jesé was given by the Spanish to the tuberose, *Polianthes tuberosa*, whose long bare stem rises several feet before its summit is thickly studded with deliciously scented flowers. Many tall and aspiring plants, like

[26]

the hollyhock and the mullein, have been linked with a Biblical character such as David or Jacob, but only the Tree of Jesse has the strange distinction of being born from glass and metal, wood, stone or textile, and the crafts that grew from the skilled hands and fertile imagination of man.

Called by the Greeks and Romans 'the mournful tree', the cypress, *Cupressus sempervirens*, was sacred to the rulers of the Underworld, and to their associates, the Fates and the Furies. It was customary to plant this tree of mourning by graves, and in the event of a death, to place it either before a house or in the vestibule. The Athenians buried their heroes in cypress coffins, believing the tree to be an emblem of immortality. Cypress branches were also used in the making of wreaths, and Sir Walter Scott wrote of this in his poem *The Cypress Wreath*:

> O, Lady, twine no wreath for me,
> Or twine it of the cypress tree!

This tree of death, strangely, became a tree of life and fertility, and Apuleius painted the son of Venus, sitting in his mother's lap, set in the midst of a cypress tree. The cypress grove on the Acropolis at Phlius in the Peloponnese was the grove where fugitives from justice became inviolable, and escaped prisoners hung upon its trees the chains for which they had no further use. It was also used as a votive tree in Mexico, from which locks of hair or teeth, and ribbons were hung.

The Persians dedicated the cypress to Mithras, their god of light and wisdom, and as such it became closely associated with fire worship, and was revered as a symbol of the sun. From its original home in the Valley of the Indus, it migrated westwards with the Iranian sun worship. It arrived very early in the Lebanon and the islands of Cyprus, which took their name from the tree. It was worshipped there as a goddess of nature. It is cultivated in India, and occasionally planted in China. The wood is scented, hard and extremely durable, and is of a permanent and beautiful red. It was considered imperishable and indestructible. It was therefore used by the Phoenicians for building ships, and in the making of costly chests for the Temple of Diana at Ephesus, and it was the wood used in the carving of the statues of the gods in the Greek temples. Precious things that were to be preserved from worms and insects were kept in cypress wood boxes, and centuries later, in *The Taming of the Shrew* (II. i), Shakespeare wrote:

> In ivory coffers I have stuff'd my crowns;
> In cypress chests my arras counterpoints,
> Costly apparel, tents, and canopies,
> Fine linen, Turkey cushions boss'd with pearl,
> Valance of Venice gold in needle-work,
> Pewter and brass, and all things that belong
> To house or housekeeping.

A Greek legend tells how Cyparissus, son of Telephus, accidentally killing Apollo's favourite stag, was so grief-stricken that he begged the gods to cause him to endure his sorrowful remorse forever. The gods answered his prayer, and he was changed into a cypress tree.

Foremost among the Christian flower symbols of the New World were the passion flowers, native to the South American forests. Superb climbing plants with intricate blooms of crimson, blue, flesh-colour, yellow and greenish-white, some bear only ornamental fruits, while other varieties are edible. In the sixteenth century, the early Spanish settlers arriving in South America saw in this remarkable bloom a marvellous emblem of Christ's passion. Its name was changed from *maracoc* or *murucuia* to the *flor de las cincollagas*, the Flower of the Five Wounds, *Flos passionis*, later to be changed by Linnaeus into *Passiflora*, the Passion flower. The pointed leaf was a symbol of the spear; the tendrils were likened to whips, and the column of the ovary to the pillar of the Cross. The stamens were thought to resemble the hammers, and the dark circle of threads – the dramatic centre of this extraordinary flower – were likened to the crown of thorns. If the flowers were white, it denoted piety, and if they were blue, heaven. The three days that are the life-span of the flower meant that 'so shall the Son of man be three days and nights in the heart of the earth'. The Jesuit fathers threw themselves with such zeal into their campaign of converting the heathen to Christianity, that artificial passion flowers were made for devotional purposes, with iron nails substituted for stigmas and a wreath of real thorns for the rays of the flower.

The flesh-coloured passion flower, *P. incarnata*, was the first to arrive in Europe, and it was introduced into England in 1629, the year of the publication of Parkinson's *Paradisi in Sole Paradisus Terrestris*. He describes the newcomer with vigorous Protestant disapproval, 'Some superstitious Jesuite would faine make me beleeve,' he writes, 'that in the flower of this plant are to be seene all the markes of our Saviours Passion . . . as thornes, nailes, whippes, pillar, etc., and all in it as true as the Sea burnes.'

The common blue passion flower, a native of Brazil, which flourishes in the open air in England, was first cultivated by the first Duchess of Beaufort, to whom we still owe so much beauty in our gardens.

The Resurrection flower, *Anastatica hierochuntica*, grows among the sands of Egypt, Arabia and Syria. When its flowers and leaves have withered and fallen off, the branches as they dry curl inwards and form a round ball. The roots die, and the plant is torn up by the winds and blown about the sands until it lodges in a damp spot, or is moistened by rain. The curled-up globe expands, and allows the seeds to drop from the seed vessels in which they had been enclosed, and they germinate. These little dried-up looking plants, if placed in a glass of water, will soon be covered with fresh buds.

The plant was believed to be propitious to nativity and, on that account, also called the Rose of the Madonna. It was placed in water by the bedside when a birth was expected, and when it had fully

The Virgin in the Bower. In mediaeval symbolism the rose
was given to Mary.

Hugo van der Goes' *Adoration of the Shepherds*, with a vase
containing a columbine with seven flowers placed before the Holy Child.

expanded it was a signal that the child was about to be born. Legends have grown round this strange plant, and it was believed to have blossomed first at Christ's birth, closed at the crucifixion, and opened again at Easter, hence its name of Resurrection flower. As for its popular name, the Rose of Jericho? It is neither a rose, nor does it grow in Jericho, and as Gerard points out, 'The coiner spoiled the name in the mint, for all plants that have been written of, there is not any more unlike the rose.'

Among the trees that blossomed to welcome Christ's birthday is the miraculous Glastonbury thorn, *Crataegus monogyna biflora*. When Joseph of Arimathea arrived on the west coast of England, the first to bring the message of the Christian faith, he landed on the Isle of Avalon, at that time a true island, but now part of the mainland. The old man, weary and despairing of the success of his mission, drove his staff, which years before had been cut from a hawthorn tree, into the ground where he and his followers came to rest, and there they knelt to pray. It was Christmas Eve, not 24 December as we know it, but 5 January, before the Gregorian calendar of 1582 had been adopted. At the words 'oh all ye green things upon the earth, bless ye the Lord', Joseph's hawthorn staff began to bud, growing as the men's voices grew with the ending of the canticle.

When the Abbey of Glastonbury was built, the hawthorn, by that time a well-rooted tree, was moved within its precincts. Parkinson, who as herborist to Queen Elizabeth and later to King James I, at a time when it was difficult to speak on such things as were labelled 'superstitions', suggested that men should not 'slightingly pass by and so smally respect this wonderful phenomenon', for it was 'a strange work of Nature, or of the God of Nature rather, to cause such a tree, being in all parts like the common Hawthorn, to blossom twice a year'.

It has been said that the life of Christ cast its shadow over the whole of the green world, and certainly the flowers which had been associated with the ancient gods slowly began to be connected in the thoughts and emotions of the people with Christ's birth and death. The monk Walafrid Strabo, the squint-eyed, who lived between 809 and 849, wrote in his *Hortulus*, 'Lilies His words were and the hallowed acts of his pleasant life, but His death re-dyed the roses.' The briar rose, *Rosa canina*, accord-ing to tradition, is the plant which formed the crown of thorns placed on Christ's brow at the crucifixion. In the early days of Christian flower symbolism, the rose stood for the blood of the martyrs. In Botticelli's 'Adoration', angels sprinkle rose petals over the Holy Child, in a garden surrounded by roses. In Hubert van Eyck's *Adoration of the Lamb*, there are bushes of roses in full bloom. In later symbolism the rose was given to Mary:

> Mystic Rose! that precious name
> Mary from the Church doth claim,

and to Dante the rose signified not only the Blessed Virgin, but the soul and centre of his faith.

The white lily, *Lilium candidum*, has been the symbol of purity in sacred art since the twelfth century, and it is dedicated to Mary in most Catholic countries. She was usually painted with a vase of flowers, or carrying a lily and a rose. Pictures of the Annunciation are few before the fourteenth century, but even in the earliest, lilies are rarely absent. Her husband, St Joseph, is also sometimes pictured with a lily in his hand, his staff, according to legend, having put forth lilies. Later artists painted the angel Gabriel with a branch of white lilies. The flower was also associated with St Catherine, for she converted her father, the Emperor Costis, by means of the madonna lily, which had been scentless until that time. When the flower miraculously gave forth its unforgettable perfume, her father was finally convinced.

The iris was the Christian emblem of royalty. A crown of irises held over the Virgin's head by angel hands; or a single iris in the hand of the Holy Child seated on the Mother's lap; or growing outside the stable; all denote the royalty of the Child born to be king.

The columbine, *Aquilegia*, with its dove-like petals, symbolizes the seven gifts of the Spirit. Since in the wild columbine there are only five petals, the early Flemish artists, always scrupulously exact, painted seven flowers on one stalk, and in Hugo van der Goes' *Adoration of the Shepherds*, a vase containing a columbine with seven flowers is placed before the Holy Child. Hubert van Eyck painted a Madonna wearing a crown of seven columbines.

Botticelli is said to have been the first artist to use the daisy, *Bellis perennis*, to symbolize the innocence of the Baby Jesus. The wild strawberry, *Fragaria*, was a sign of righteousness, and the violet of humility, and both are seen in Botticelli's pictures.

The greatest botanist of the sixteenth century, Caspard Bauhin, was probably the first to collect together a Sacred Flora in 1591. This, although small, made valuable groundwork for the future. It was followed in 1630 by the work of an Italian physician, Ambrosini, founded on Bauhin but not extending his researches. A doctor of French descent, Du Val, wrote in 1643 another Sacred Flora, again with no original work, but aimed at explaining Bauhin's ideas, and for more than 200 years no further works appeared. It was only by consulting general books on plant names, and comparing these with those of other countries, that it was discovered what a vast and beautiful Flora had existed among Christian nations.

Geoffrey Grigson, in his *Englishman's Flora*, first published in 1958, lists more than seventy Lady flowers, offered with love, warmth and often fun, for Her needs – a loan or a gift from any mother to the One Mother. Lady's Petticoat, the delicate Wood Anemone, *Anemone nemorosa*, was Hers, and Lady's Buttons, the Greater Stitchwort, *Stellaria holostea*, as well as the freedom of Lady's Bunch of Keys, the Cowslip, *Primula veris*. Such anachronisms as Lady's

Hatpins, Field Scabious, *Knautia arvensis*; Lady's
Umbrella, and even Lady's Shimmy, both names
given to the same plant, the Larger Bindweed, *Caly-
stegis sepium*, are all Hers today.

From the thirteenth century the custom grew of
displaying in churches and homes scenes of the
Christmas crib, with Joseph and Mary, the Holy
Child and as many figures as could be arranged in the
space available. Sometimes a legend would be illustrated, such as that of Madalon, the shepherd girl
offering a wreath of roses to the Baby Christ. The
figures were often beautifully modelled and richly
dressed, and prominent artists were engaged to
design the groups and paint the scenery. The manu-
facture of these stable groups in France and
Germany, and particularly in Naples, grew into prosperous industries, and many churches had regular
endowments for their maintenance.

Great care was taken in choosing the herbs that
filled the cradle, where nowadays the bedding and
the fodder would only be hay and straw. Each plant,
and the flowering grasses, downy seeds and soft
mosses, was placed in the crib for its symbolism or
perhaps its special fragrance, and these wild flowers
were given names appropriate to their use. Collec-
tively, they were known as cradle-grasses, cradle-
worts, or Holy Hay. Legends grew about the flowers
and names were given that still remain, although
their meanings may have been forgotten.

Sage of Bethlehem, for instance, was the name
given in Lincolnshire for garden mint, *Mentha
viridis*, which marks it as their cradle-wort. All the
mints were dedicated to Mary in France, Germany
and Italy, as well as in Britain, and garden mint,
according to Gerard, was known as Our Lady's
Mint. In Italy, a smaller mint was chosen, the
Pulegium, which was given the name of Brother-
wort. Its potent scent when bruised led to its being
employed in strewing the paths of processions, or the
floors of banqueting halls, and hence it was also
known as Churchwort or Bishopswort. There was a

Garden mint, from a fourteenth-century manuscript. In mediaeval times all the varieties of mint were dedicated to the Virgin Mary.

tradition that if the *Pulegium* was gathered at day-break on the Feast of St John the Baptist on 24 June, and kept until the Nativity, it would naturally dry up; but if it is placed upon the altar at which the first Mass is to be sung that night, the dry herb would revive.

The old botanical name of *Cunilago* or Cradle-wort for the wild thyme, *Thymus serpillum*, is proof enough if we require it, that it is one of the Nativity plants. The seeds of the common sow-thistle, *Sonchus oleraceus*, supplied the silky down for the Baby to lie on, and this, according to Gerard, was called St Maries seeds, and it is known (*The Flora of the Nativity* by Alfred E. P. Raymond Dowling) to grow in Bethlehem.

The collective names of Cradle-grass, Cradle-wort and Holy Hay are forgotten now, but the wild flowers are still growing, although in sadly diminishing numbers, and their legends linger on.

[35]

The strange and wonderful

Although many trees and flowers are strange enough in their own forms and properties, the imagination of man, unsatisfied with reality, has frequently invented fantasy plants, or enlarged upon those already existing; bestowing good or evil powers that might have surprised even nature herself.

The loneliest of all trees, the Arabian tree, was imagined to shelter the phoenix, a mythological bird; and both may be considered to have a literary existence, if not a physical one. It was the custom of the phoenix when its course was ended (anything from 500 to 1461 years, it was said), and death hovered near, to build its nest in the Arabian tree, and there deposit the Principles of Life, from which a new progeny arose.

To believe in the phoenix is to believe in the Arabian tree, for neither would have existed without the other. Shakespeare wrote of both in *The Phoenix and the Turtle*:

> Let the bird of loudest lay
> On the sole Arabian tree,
> Herald sad, and trumpet be
> To whose sound chaste wings obey.

In *The Tempest* III.iii, he also makes Sebastian, lost on a magical island, say as a token of his disbelief:

> now I will believe
> That there are unicorns; that in Arabia
> There is one tree, the phoenix' throne; one phoenix
> At this hour reigning there.

Sir Thomas Browne puts a neat end to the myth of the phoenix, and therefore to the Arabian tree; 'in as much as there were no single creatures in the Ark, only pairs, [so that] earthly existence could not have

The 'Goose-Barnacle Tree' from Gerard's *Historie of Plants* (1597)

been possible.' However, nebulous legend became embroidered fact. 'In the south countree is a manere palm that is alone in that kynde; and none other spryngeth ayen of itself; and therefore men trow that the Fenix that is a byrde of Arabia, hath the name of the palme of Arabia.' The legendary phoenix sank back into its own ashes to be seen no more, but the Arabian tree became identified with the acacia, on which the people of Mecca hung weapons, garments, ostrich eggs and other offerings at an annual pilgrimage. Yet another Arabian tree, the sacred date-palm, was also honoured at a yearly feast, and hung with fine clothes and women's ornaments. Both legendary bird and living tree have been made emblems of immortality.

The fabulous goose-barnacle tree was best described by Gerard, who concludes his *Historie of Plants* (1597):

with the naked and bare truth, though unpolished. There are found in the North parts of Scotland and the islands adjacent, called Orchades, certaine trees where-

The legendary Phoenix, from a fourteenth-century herbal.

on do grow certaine shells of a white colour tending to russett, wherein are contained little living things, which shells in time of maturitie do open, and out of them do grow those little living creatures, which falling in the water do become fowles, which we call Barnackles, and in Lancashire tree-geese.

An eye-witness account from Lancashire describes the birth of this remarkable bird-plant as:

a certaine spawne or froth that in time breedeth unto certaine shels, in shape like those of a muskle, but sharper-pointed wherein is contained a thing in forme like a lace of silke finely woven together as it were. One end thereof is fastened into a rude masse or lumpe, which in time cometh to the shape or forme of a Birde. When it is perfectly formed the shel gapeth open, and the first thing that appeareth is the foresaid lace or string: next come the legs of the bird hanging out, and as it groweth greater it openeth the shel by degrees til at length it is all come forth and hangeth only by the bill: In short space after it cometh to full maturitie, it falleth into the sea, when it gathereth feathers and groweth to a Fowle bigger than a Mallard and lesser than a Goose, having blacke legs and bill and beake, and feathers blacke and white, spotted in such manner as is our magpie.

Similar creatures were seen on the seashore near Dover, and so common they were, it is said, that a good specimen could be bought for threepence. Seeing is believing, we are told, but would not believing is seeing come as near to the truth?

The fourteenth-century writer Sir John Maundeville said, 'In our country were trees that bear a fruit that becomes flying birds; those that fell in the water lived, and those that fell on the earth died, and these be right good for man's meat.'

A Scottish historian wrote that these barnacle-geese were first produced in the form of worms in old trees, and that such a tree was cast on shore in 1480, and when it was sawn asunder, a multitude of worms 'throwing themselves out of sundry holes and pores of the tree; some of them were nude as they were new shapen; some had head, feet, and wings, but they had no feathers; some of them were perfect shapen fowls. At last, the people having this tree each day in more admiration, brought it to the kirk of St. Andrew's, beside the town of Tyre, where it yet remains to our day' – but possibly not to ours.

First mentioned in the twelfth century, these minutely described and frequently illustrated bird-fishes or fish-birds, born of trees, apparently haunted the eastern coasts of England and Scotland, until incredulity gradually whispered doubts into unwilling ears, and a traveller chancing to be in Scotland enquired particularly for the place of the wonderful metamorphosis of the Barnacle, but was referred to the remote Hebrides and Orkneys, 'but as he sought to advance the miracle retired from him'.

The strange fruit known as the Apple of Sodom is found on the desolate shores of the Dead Sea, on the site of the twin cities of Sodom and Gomorrah, upon which 'the Lord rained brimstone and fire' because of the sin and corruption of their inhabitants. Its first appearance, it is said, is always attended with a bitter north-east wind, and 'therefore ships of the Black Sea take care to sail before the harbinger of bad weather comes forth'.

This is the Ethiopian Apple of some of the old herbalists, and indeed it does grow in Ethiopia. In his *Voiage and Travaile of John Maundeville*, Sir John Maundeville claims, 'There be full faire apples, and fair of colour to behold; but whoso breaketh them in two, he shall find within them coals and cinders, in token that by the wrath of God, the city and the land were burnt and sunken into hell.' Another of the ominous names of this shrub is the Dead Sea Fruit, and a traveller by the name of Henry Teonge, visiting the country round the Dead Sea in 1675, described it as being 'all over full of stones which look like burnt syndurs and on some low shrubs there grow small round things which are called Apples, but no witt like them. They are somewhat fair to look at, but touch them and they smoulder all to black ashes like soot both for looks and smell.'

The name now belongs to a shrub of the night-shade family, *Solanum sodomeum*, an egg-plant bearing yellow tomato-like fruit, subject to attacks of a species of *Cynips*, an insect which punctures the rind, and converts the interior of the fruit into ashes, leaving the outside whole and untouched. It is considered a symbol of sin in the Near East.

The *Dracaena draco* or Dragon-tree, derives its name from the Greek *Drakaina*, a female dragon. It is found in the East India Islands, the Canaries, Cape Verde and Sierra Leone. Gerard described it as 'This strange and admirable tree ... resembling the Pine-tree'. Among its leaves:

> come forth little mossie floures, of small moment, and turn into berries of the bignesse of Cherries, of a yellowish colour, round, light, and bitter, covered with a three-fold skin, or film, wherein is to be seen ... the form of a dragon, having a long neck and gaping

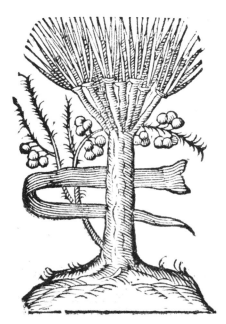

The 'Dragon Tree' of Orotava, from a seventeenth-century herbal.

mouth, the ridge, or back, armed with sharp prickles like the porcupine, with a long taile and foure feet, very easie to be discerned of. . . . The trunk, or body of the tree, is covered with a tough bark, very thin and easie to be opened or wounded with any small toole or instrument; which being so wounded in the dog days, bruised or bored, yields forth drops of a thick red liquour of the name of the tree called Dragon's Tears, or *Sanguis draconis,* Dragon's Bloud.

The famous and venerable Dragon-tree of Orotava was for many centuries worshipped as a sacred tree by the original inhabitants of the Canary Islands, the Guanches, who used its resin for embalming in the Egyptian manner. It was considered one of the wonders of the island of Tenerife. It has long ago been destroyed by successive storms, but in 1799, a traveller wrote, 'Its trunk is divided into a great number of branches, which rise in the form of candelabra, and are terminated by tufts of leaves like the Yucca: it still bears every year both leaves and fruit . . . an inexhaustible source of motion and of life.'

In the South Sea Islands it was considered to be a most potent magic plant, and was brought by the Venetian merchants to Europe, where it was used by deserted medieval wives and maidens as a love philtre. If it was burned near an open window for seven consecutive midnights, the fumes would bring back a straying husband or lover, always supposing that a substitute had not answered the invitation in a lesser time. Widely differing species of this tree are to be found in China, and parts of South America, and many have medicinal uses. The *Dracaena draco* shares with the baobab tree the distinction of being the oldest living representative of the vegetable kingdom.

The Indian Sad Tree, *Nyctanthes arbortristis*, is a species of jasmine, whose deliciously scented flowers open at sunset and fall at dawn, so that the sad sight it presents during the daylight hours has given it the name of the Tree of Sorrow. Both in appearance and perfume it resembles orange or lemon blossom, and was frequently used in temples. The ladies of Batavia, on evening visits, wore the flowers threaded on a string, as a wreath. Each day the fresh buds were brought to the markets for sale, in preparation for their opening at sunset.

In Goa the tree is called Parizataco, after a Governor whose beautiful daughter fell in love with the sun. The blasé sun, all too used to the adoration of beautiful maidens, predictably tired of the girl, who killed herself in her despair. Over her grave grew a night jasmine, the Tree of Sorrow, whose flowers, having such a horror of the sun, refused to open in its presence. In memory of the broken-hearted daughter of Parizataco, the Sad Tree stands by day, with leaves apparently lifeless, withered and scentless until night comes to revive it.

The elder tree, *Sambucus nigra*, in whatever part of the world it may be found, is a tree of magic, and the old story spread by Sir John Maundeville that there stood in the vicinity of Mount Sion 'the tre of the eldre, that Judas henge himself upon, for

The Indian 'Sad Tree', or Tree of Sorrow.

despeyr, that he hadde, when he solde and betrayed our Lord', has long since given way to happier folklore.

In Denmark its name is associated with Hulda or Hilda, the Elder Mother or Elder Queen who lived in its root, and was the good mother of the elves; and thus the tree was made her symbol. Should anyone wish to cut down an elder tree, or even a branch, he first had to ask permission of the Elder Mother, otherwise some misfortune would befall him. The floorboards and furniture should never be made of her wood, and even a cradle was inadvisable, for the Elder Mother would come and pull the infant out by its legs. However, on the night of 6 January, one might cut a branch from the tree after permission was asked, and spit three times if it was not given. Making a magic circle with the branch in some lonely field, one may then demand of the devil some of his precious fern seed, that gives the possessor the strength of thirty men. Hulda will then see that the fern seed, wrapped in a chalice cloth is brought by an unseen hand. As well as supplying a superabundance of masculine strength, fern seed keeps worms out of furniture, fends off snakes and mosquitoes, and cures toothache.

In Russia elders prolong life, and they were used to keep out evil spirits. In the Tyrol, a young elder-bush cut in the form of a cross was planted on a newly dug grave. If it bloomed, it meant that the soul of the dead was in Paradise. In Germany the pith of the branches was cut into flat round shapes, dipped in oil, lighted and put to float in a glass of water. On Christmas Eve this would reveal all the witches and sorcerers in the neighbourhood, if it was desired on such a night.

English summer arrives with the elder and departs with the ripening of its berries, and like the rowan it, too, was a guardian tree. Planted beside a farm or cottage it kept away lightning, as well as witches and wizards, and in Sussex an elder twig with three or four knots in it was carried in the pocket as a charm against rheumatism. Farm carts were drawn by horses whose bridles were decorated with elder flowers to keep away the flies, a precaution that obviously did not include black-fly, which settle on the flower-stalks in their thousands towards the end of their blooming period. There was a pleasant country belief that if the flowers were put into ale, and a man and woman drank it together, they would be married within a year.

A kind of Pan-pipe was made from the stem, and Pliny records the belief that the shrillest sounds were made from elder trees which grew out of the sound of cock-crow. Toy battles, too, could be fought with its aid, and Nicholas Culpeper (1616–54), author of the famous *Herbal*, said of the elder that 'It is needless to write any description of this, since every boy that plays with a pop-gun will not mistake another tree for the elder.'

It had, and still has, many uses in medicine, especially in homœopathy. John Evelyn wrote that 'If the medicinal properties of its leaves, bark and berries were fully known, I cannot tell what our countryman could ail for which he might not fetch a remedy from any hedge, either for sickness or wounds.'

Saints and their seasons

Flowers are often dedicated to or named after saints. The choice of these flowers was usually governed by their availability at the time of the saint's feast, and it would have been an added favour if the plant possessed healing properties as well. Sometimes the flowers grew or were planted near the saint's shrine. The adoption of the saints dates back to the fourth century, when the custom of dedicating churches to patron saints arose from the practice of building churches over the tombs of martyrs. The following are only a few of the many saints with their feast days and flowers:

13 January St Hilary, Bishop and Confessor, had for his plant the barren strawberry, *Fragaria sterilis*. He was Bishop of Poitiers, and champion of the orthodox doctrine against the Arians. He died in 367. The first law term in the year, the Hilary term, is called after this saint.

3 February St Blaise, Bishop and Martyr. Bishop of Sebaste in Cappadocia, he was a man of great learning who was put to death by Agricolus in 316. He is the patron saint of the wool-combers, and all the mills of Yorkshire had a holiday on his feast, everyone carrying thistles in lieu of teasels. Parson Woodforde describes the Grand Procession of Bishop Blaise which took place on the saint's day in the streets of Norwich in 1783: 'The grand Procession began about 11 o'clock this morning ...' The procession, headed by Four Trumpeters, included The Golden Fleece and Jason, a reference to the wool-combers, with no less than forty Argonauts, as well as the good Bishop in a Phaeton drawn by six horses, and 'the book-keepers, Shepherds and Shepherdesses belonging to the different Societies of Combers, seven Companies on foot and five Companies on Horseback . . . Hercules, Jason, and Bishop Blaise, were exceedingly well kept up and very superbly dressed. All the Combers wore white ruffled shirts with Cross-Belts of Wool of divers Colours – with Mitred Caps on their heads – The Shepherds and Shepherdesses were little Boys and Girls on horseback, very handsomely and [with] great Propriety dressed.' He does not mention whether anyone carried the Great Water Moss, which is the saint's flower.

1 March St David, Archbishop of Menevia. He was of the Royal family of the Britons, uncle to the great King Arthur, son of Xanthus, Prince of Wales. He died about 642. He is offered either the leek or the daffodil.

23 April St George, Martyr. Patron saint of England. He was born in Cappadocia and died for the sake of his religion in 290, under the Emperor Diocletian. His fight with the dragon is symbolical of the triumph of the Christian hero over the power of evil. It was the custom to wear bluebells on St George's day, and also to decorate the churches.

19 May St Dunstan, Archbishop of Canterbury. Born in Glastonbury about 924. This worthy painter, jeweller and blacksmith held the devil by the nose with his red-hot pincers until he promised never to tempt him again. One night Dunstan dreamed of an immense tree, whose branches stretched all over Britain, its boughs loaded with countless cowls, the top crowned with a cowl larger than all the others. The tree, as Dunstan interpreted his dream, was the England of the future. He was given the monkshood, *Aconitum napellus*, as his flower, a symbol derived from his prophetic dream.

St Swithin, from the tenth-century *Benedictional of St Ethelwold*. His flower is the Cape marigold.

St George, who slayed a dragon to save the life of the King of Selena's daughter, Princess Sabra, and so won the king and his people over to Christianity.

24 June St Alban, England's first Christian martyr, and said to have been the first Grand Master of the Freemasons. Born at Verulam, then a Roman colony, now known as St Albans. He gave up his life for his friend Amphibalus, a Christian priest, and was be-headed on a hill overlooking Verulam. As Wordsworth said:

> Thus was St. Alban tried,
> England's first martyr, whom no threats could shake.
> Self-offered victim for his friend he died,
> And for the faith.

15 July St Swithin, Bishop of Winchester. He died in 862 and expressed a wish before dying that he might be buried in the cemetery, and not in the church as bishops always were, so that the rain might drop on his grave; thinking 'no vault so good as the vault of heaven'. The monks wished to remove his body, but were compelled to relinquish the idea in consequence of the heavy rain which lasted for forty days. Thus arose the belief that if it rains on St Swithin's day, it will rain for forty days and forty nights after. His flower is the small Cape marigold, *Calendula pluvialis*, and he himself was known as Weeping St Swithin.

28 August St Augustine, Bishop of Hippo. Born at Targasta in Numidia, in 354, of a Christian mother and a pagan father. His flower is the golden rod, *Solidago virgaurea*.

1 September St Giles, Abbot. He was born in Athens and died in 795. He travelled to France, having first sold his estates and given the proceeds to charity. He is the patron saint of beggars and cripples. Most churches named in his honour are situated at the entrance of towns, where once beggars used to gather. His flower is the St Giles' orpine, *Sedum telephium*.

25 October St Crispin, Martyr. Crispinus and Crispianus were two brothers born in Rome. During

ABOVE LEFT:
St Dunstan, Archbishop of Canterbury in the tenth century,
was given the monkshood as his symbolic flower.

ABOVE RIGHT:
St Alban was England's first Christian martyr, and said
to have been the first Grand Master of the Freemasons.

their travels to spread the Gospel they supported
themselves by shoe-making. They were both be-
headed for their faith in Soissons in the year 308.
There is a tradition in the Romney Marsh that the
relics of these saints were cast into the sea, and
washed ashore on the Kentish coast, and public
houses have been called the Crispin, or St Crispin or
Crispin and Crispianus, after them. Only Crispin has
been given a flower, fleabane starwort, *Aster
conizoides*, but both are honoured on the day of the
battle of Agincourt, 1415.

> And Crispin Crispian shall ne'er go by,
> From this day to the ending of the world,
> But we in it shall be remembered, –
>
> *Henry V*, Act IV, Scene III

25 November St Catherine, Virgin and Martyr. She
was born in Alexandria, and in about 305 was converted to Christianity, which she professed with

great courage and constancy, until she met her death by the torture of a wheel stuck with spikes, rolled over her body. She was afterwards beheaded. In an essay by Antoine Houdant de la Motte (1672–1731), published in London in 1730, he says 'St Catherine is esteemed in the Church of Rome as a Saint and Patroness of Spinsters; and her holiday is observed, not in Popish countries only, but even in many places in this nation: young women meeting on the 25th of November and making merry together, which they call Catherning.' Her fatal wheel, the Catherine wheel, is also with complete irrelevance one of the features of Guy Fawkes night on 5 November. Her flower was once the sweet butter burr, *Petasites vulgaris*, but it has been changed for the love-in-a-mist, *Nigella damascena*, which is sometimes called St Catherine's flower, since its surrounding linear foliage bears some resemblance to a wheel.

6 December St Nicholas, Bishop of Myra. He died in 343. He was made patron saint of boys and young sailors in Greece, and in England of the Worshipful Company of Parish Clerks of the City of London. Saint Nikölaas or Klaas was of Dutch ancestry, much loved for his secret gifts to the young and poor. The custom of giving presents secretly on the Eve of St Nicholas, 6 December, travelled with the Dutch settlers to New England, where Sant Klaas became Santa Claus. In England his gift-giving was moved to Christmas Eve and his duties were taken over by Father Christmas. Sadly, no one remembers to leave a sprig of nest-flowered heath, *Erica nidiflora*, the flower of St Nicholas, at the end of the bed on Christmas Eve as an acknowledgement of the good old man's beneficence.

Christmas flowers

The winter aconite, *Eranthis hyemalis*, is rather too small and comes perhaps too late to decorate our houses for Christmas, but to the French it is still the *rose de Noël*, as it was when the herbalist William Coles wrote his *Art of Simpling* in 1656. 'Very wonderful effects may be wrought by the Vertues, which are enveloped within the compasse of the Green Mantles wherein many Plants are adorned', he said, and whether or no the green mantle of the winter aconite can work any medicinal miracles, it is one of the most attractive little wrappings that ever flower was equipped with in which to brave the chills of winter. Perhaps we should describe it as a ruff rather than a mantle, though botanists would call it neither, but it sets off the bright yellow of its sunny countenance to perfection. It is the *Christwurzel* of the Germans.

The ivy, *Hedera helix*, holds its yellow-green flowers, with their minute calyx teeth, from the time they unfold in late October, all through November and December, until the handsome black or deep purple berries form. The flowers have little scent, but they yield an abundance of nectar, the last the year has to offer to the bees. Ivy will only produce flowers when the branches rise above their support, and the leaves lose their five lobes and become ovate; and therefore low-creeping ivy will never bloom. The berries do not ripen until the spring, although they provide food for the birds during winter. Today its handsome leaves are used for Christmas decoration in church and home, though it makes no appearance in Christmas lore and legend. Perhaps this is because it was once forbidden because of the plant's pagan associations with Bacchus, to whom it was dedicated; ivy was bound round the head to prevent intoxication. English taverns used to display the sign of an ivy bush over their doors, which indicated the excellence of the supplies within; hence the saying, 'Good wine needs no bush.'

Popular as a Christmas flower now, although unknown at one time in English homes, the poinsettia, a species of *Euphorbia*, displays its fiery burst of scarlet bracts when colour is most needed. In Spain it is known as the *Flor de Noche Buena*, the Flower of the Holy Night, and its flaming star is one of the most striking emblems of the star of Bethlehem that we may see. Nevertheless, the fact that it may only be produced under glass in this country seems to make it still a stranger in our midst at Christmas.

Our own native Christmas rose is beautiful, dependable and sturdy. Its old name of Melampode comes from Melampus, a physician who, in about 1400 BC, used it to cure the mad daughters of Prœtus, King of Argus; it therefore acquired a tremendous reputation as a cure for insanity. It was used to purify houses, and to drive away evil spirits, and it is regarded as the emblem of purity. It is called *Helleborus niger*, the black hellebore, because of its black root. Tradition tells how this little snow rose first grew in the gardens of heaven, and was looked after by the angels, who called it the rose of love. At the Fall, when Paradise lay shrouded in snow, and of all the flowers tended by Adam and Eve not one remained in Eden, the angels asked God to let them carry to earth this small white flower as a token of His love and mercy:

> Since when this winter rose
> Blossoms amid the snows,
> A symbol of God's promise, care and love.
>
> Anon.

Better known is the story of the shepherd girl Madelon, who came to Bethlehem to see for herself the miracle. She was very poor, and she wept that there was not one flower in that winter landscape for her to pick and offer to the Child. God, seeing her distress, sent Gabriel to her, who said, 'Madelon, what makes you weep while you pray?', and taking her by the hand, led her out into the dark night. Then he touched the frozen earth with his staff, and on every side there sprang up the white flowers of the Christmas rose. This is why we may see in many pictures of the Holy Family a vase of Christmas roses.

Although their flowers have matured into berries by Christmas-time, both holly and mistletoe must surely have a place among the few green things that gladden our cold winter days. The holly tree was known to a mediaeval monks as the Holy tree, and as such it was believed to have the power of keeping away evil spirits. Many old houses have a holly tree planted nearby, in the added belief that it also protects from lightning. Christians were not the first people to garland their houses with holly. The Romans used it to decorate their halls during the midwinter festival of the Saturnalia. They also exchanged gifts as we do, and with these they sent sprigs of holly as tokens of good will. Holly has separate male and female trees, and the male tree will never produce berries. It is the emblem of Eternal Life, sometimes called Christ's Thorn, and its thorny leaves and scarlet berries are understood as symbols of Christ's suffering. It should not be introduced into the house before Christmas Eve, and must be removed on Twelfth Night.

Many years ago it was customary among the Germans, on one of the sacred nights of the winter festival, to go out and cut branches from the hedgerows. These were brought home, put into water, or planted in a pot of moist earth, and kept in the open air or in the house. A month later each branch would be in full leaf or bloom, and it was then carried round among friends or relations, to touch with the branch anybody to whom one wished to bring health, strength and fruitfulness. Those touched with the

CHRISTMAS FLOWERS

ABOVE LEFT:
Christmas roses in a Victorian painting by William Dobson.
There is a legend that the Angel Gabriel caused the flowers to
grow in the frozen winter earth so that a poor shepherd girl
could give them as a gift to the Holy Child.

ABOVE RIGHT:
An Edwardian personification of winter. The legends surrounding
mistletoe originate with the ancient Druids and the myths of Scandinavia.

BELOW:
Holly decorating a children's bedroom in a Victorian Christmas card.
In mediaeval times holly was known as the 'Holy tree', and was believed
to have the power of keeping away evil spirits.

holy branch would present the striker with gifts. The custom survived on the Continent as a children's game.

Mistletoe is a plant of curious lore and mystery. Shakespeare called it 'baleful', perhaps in allusion to the Scandinavian legend of Balder the Beautiful, the god of Peace, accidentally slain with an arrow made of mistletoe, the only wood to which he was vulnerable. He was restored to life at the request of the other gods and goddesses, and the mistletoe was given into the keeping of the goddess of Love, and it was ordained that everyone who passed under its branches should receive a kiss, to show that mistletoe had become an emblem of love and not of hate. How many kisses have been given and received, or shall we say exchanged, since then, and what changes of mood, from the golden boy lying slain among his fellow gods, to the fun and games under the kissing bunch, and back again to tragedy with the ballad of *The Mistletoe Bough*, inevitably sung each Victorian Christmas! In this, a young bride, happily joining in a game of hide-and-seek, conceals herself in an old oak chest, whose lid closes with a spring. The opening lines, so familiar to our grandparents, set the scene:

> The mistletoe hung in the castle hall
> The holly-bush shone on the old oak wall,

and the refrain of 'Oh, the mistletoe bough!' echoed for an epoch through parlours if not castle halls, for many an otherwise festive season. Compared with these, the ceremonies of the white-clad Druids, cutting their sacred mistletoe with a golden sickle, and sacrificing two white bullocks, amid 'orasions and prayers', seem to us as pale ghosts from another world than this.

Elf-shot and evil eye

To the Anglo-Saxons, the doctrine of Elf-shot was of the greatest importance, and the longest chapter in the third book of the tenth-century Leech Book of Bald was entirely against 'elf-disease'. Unaccountable deaths or sickness in animals and humans, and there were many, were believed to be the direct result of 'Elf-shot'. Small flint arrowheads, now known to have been made by Neolithic man, were attributed to elves – no red-capped pixies either, but unseen, unheard creatures of hate and malice. The germs and viruses that laid low Stone Age man and his cattle, left solid evidence, or so they believed. When no physical shot was to be seen, it was assumed that the arrowhead made no wound, but instead caused paralysis. We still use the word 'stroke' in the sense of a paralytic seizure, unaware that it originally meant 'Elf-stroke'. When no wounds were to be seen to account for the sickness of the animal, there were usually men or women who pretended to feel it in the flesh, and undertook a cure by incantation. A needle would be folded in a leaf taken from the prayer book and fastened into the hair of the cow. Not only was this supposed to cure the cow, but it also served as a charm against further attacks. In a *Survey of Southern Ireland*, the writer says, 'I have seen one of these elf-stones like a thin triangular flint, not half an inch in diameter, with which they suppose these fairies destroy their cows.'

> There ev'ry herd by sad experience knows
> How, wing'd with fate, their elf-shot arrows fly,
> When this sick ewe his summer food forgoes,
> Or stretch'd on earth the heart-smit heifers lie.

John Brand, *Popular Antiquities*, 1813

These Elf-arrows had shafts of reeds, and carefully sharpened flints which were adjusted so as to detach themselves from the shaft and remain in the wounded body. Their purpose was for hunting, or to be used in battle, others being made for tools and daily use. Usually plants that break easily, such as stitchwort, were used as a cure for Elf-shot wounds, and stitchwort was known to be an elf-plant.

Herbs used as amulets as well as in medicine were employed against the Evil Eye, a threat of the unknown against man and his cattle, more anciently recorded and more widely feared than Elf-shot. *Helleborus niger* was dug up with many religious ceremonies to bless the cows and sheep; thus Virgil in his *Pastorals*:

> What magic has bewitched the woolly dams,
> And what ill-eyes behind the tender lambs?

and cows which had lost their milk were known to have been 'overlooked'. Everywhere that dairy produce was tampered with, livestock injured, and human beings visited with sickness or death, was known to be assailed by the Evil Eye. In Italy a sprig of juniper was hung over every stable. There were, however, other methods of warding off this everpresent menace. Many plants diverted evil by means of their smell, such as lilies, artemisia and mugwort. In some cases they were burned as incense, in others hung at doors and windows. Onions, garlic, leeks and chives were known to be efficacious. An onion, if suspended in a room, possessed the magical power of attracting and absorbing maladies that would otherwise attack the inmates. Sandalwood was used for exorcism. The elder was thought to be a protective plant, and so was planted near houses. It was vulnerable, however, and known to bleed if it was cut. Mistletoe was an anti-witch plant, welcomed when it grew of itself in apple trees. Rosemary was a countercharm, used at weddings and funerals.

Colour, too, could be a potent charm, and of all colours, red was the most valued. All over the world we find things of a red colour used for protection. In China charms were tied with red string, written on red paper, or printed in red ink. Red silk was tied round a baby's wrist, and old and young regarded red as the best safeguard of all against the Evil Eye. At the New Year the Cantonese would clear out their houses, and post near the doors a pair of scrolls made of red paper, on which was an inscription naming some magic plant, such as, 'The Sweet-flag, like a sword, destroys a thousand evil influences.' On the birth of a son, a Brahman father, having banished the women from the room, would take the new baby and place on its head some red-coloured rice as a protection. Scottish Highlanders would tie red thread round the tails of their cattle, and women wore red silk or wool round a finger. A prescription against headache advises waybroad (plantain), which had to be dug up without iron before sunrise, 'with a red fillet'. Even the robin was regarded with reverence because of his red breast. But the strongest charm of all was the combination of rowan tree (mountain ash), with its scarlet berries, and red thread:

> Rowan-tree and red thread,
> Put the witches to their speed.

Ancient country saying

Red was the colour sacred to Thor, and it was abhorred by the powers of darkness and evil.

In the *Herbarium of Apuleius* of the eleventh century, mugwort, *Artemisia vulgaris*, was advised; 'and if a root of this wort be hung over the door of any house there may not any man damage the house.' Birthwort (*Aristolochia*) was also recommended against the Evil Eye, as well as alyssum, horehound, peony, vervain, yarrow and betony. William Coles said in 1656 that if the roots of angelica were carried about a man he would be protected from evil.

> Contagious aire ingendring Pestilence
> Infects not those that in the mouth have ta'en
> Angelica, that happy counterbane.

Mrs C. F. Leyel, The Magic of Herbs, 1932

ABOVE:
May Day in 1812, by William Collins. Plants such as ragwort and whitethorn were traditionally gathered on the first day in May and hung in the entrances to houses to ward off witches and evil spirits.

Aristolochia Serpentaria

Published by Phillips & London, Dec'r 1st 1831.

LEFT:
Birthwort, from William Woodville's *Medical Botany* of 1832. This was one of several plants recommended for use against the Evil Eye.

Snapdragon with its snapping jaws acted as a counter-charm, and so did cinquefoil, valerian and rue. Ragwort, although a witch-plant, was used with equal success against them, and whitethorn, gathered on Mayday, was hung in the entries of houses. Highland women often carried a piece of the root of groundsel in their pocket against the Evil Eye. The young scroll-like fronds of the male fern, *Filix mas*, were sought for and treasured when found, for they were known to be a protection against sorcery, and on St John's Eve every man's house was decorated with green birch, long fennel, orpine, white lilies and, of course, St John's wort. Its other name of hypericum comes from a Greek word meaning 'to protect'. Hyssop, too, was hung in houses and used with various ceremonials as a great cleanser:

> O, who can tell
> The hidden pow'r of herbes and might of magic spell?
>
> Anon.

Perhaps a description of part of the contents of a city pharmacy of the sixteenth century may give a sense of reality to this world of strange belief. 'In large wooden boxes were stored the dried leaves, flowers, seeds, bark and roots of many aromatic herbs, including saffron, ginger, elder, wormwood, borage, rhubarb, aloes, jalap, rue, Abyssinian myrrh, Solomon's seal, and St John's wort, gathered on St John's Day and much in demand for expelling evil spirits from sick persons.'

Today when we think we have 'caught' a cold, may not the cold have caught us – directed maybe by Elf-shot, or 'overlooked' by the Evil Eye?

The star-eyed science

The theory of Astrological Botany was founded in the belief that the ways of men and of plants were influenced by the stars. 'There is not an herbe here below, but he hath a star in Heaven above, and the star strikes him with her beames, and says to him "Grow!",' wrote Thomas Vaughan.

Even when the Saxons first went to gather their healing herbs they believed that the plants must be picked at sunrise, or when day and night divided, looking towards the east, and turning 'as the sun goeth from east to south and west'.

Paracelsus (a name coined for himself by Theophrastus Bombastus von Hohenheim) lived between 1493 and 1541, and was full of enthusiasm and somewhat confused botanical mysticism. He held that each star was a spiritualized plant and each plant a terrestrial star – a theory that must have made the practice of the early herbalists more than a little obscure.

'Picking medicinal herbs must be done when the moon is in the sign of the Virgin, and not when Jupiter is in the ascendant, for then the herb loses its virtue,' Anthony Askham wrote in the sixteenth century. 'Asterion or Lunary groweth among stoones and in high places, this herb shyneth by night and he bringeth forth purple floures hole and rounde as a knockebell or else lyke to foxgloves, the leves of this herbe be rounde and blew and they have the mark of the Moone in the myddes as it were thre leved grasse, but the leves thereof be more, and they be round as a peny. And the stalk of this herb is red and thyse herb semeth as it were musk and the juyce thereof is yelow and this groweth in the new Moone without leve to the end of fyftene dayes and after fyftene dayes it looseth every day a leave as the Moone waneth and it springeth and waneth as doth the Moone and where that it groweth there groweth great quantitie.'

Francis Bacon, not uncritical of this botanical stardust, stated his views with his usual clarity: 'Some of the Ancients, and likewise divers of the Moderne Writers, that have laboured in *Naturall Magick*, have noticed a *Sympathy*, between the *Sunne*, *Moone*, and some Principal *Starres*; and certain Herbs, and *Plants*. And so they have denominated some *Herbs Solar*, and some *Lunar*; and such like Toyes put into great Words.'

The East Anglian farmer, Thomas Tusser, had clear guidelines in his *Five Hundred Points of Good Husbandrie* (1562):

> Sow peason and beanes in the wane of the moone,
>> Who soweth them sooner, he soweth too soone,
> That they with the planet may rest and arise,
>> And flourish with bearing most plentiful wise.

Not only plants, but men were moon-governed, according to Charles Estienne in 1569. 'The farmer shall not be content to know what force and efficacy every quarter of the moon hath upon beasts, trees, plants, herbs, fruit, and other things: but shall also be carefull to observe what powers every day of the moon hath not only upon beast and plant, but also in the disposition and government of man.'

Even John Aubrey agreed that 'if a plant be not gathered according to the rules of astrology, it hath little or no virtue in it', and John Woolridge was positive that he had the answer to the doubling of flowers. 'The seeds from which you expect to have double Flowers, must be sown at the Full of the Moon or in two or three days after. It hath been long

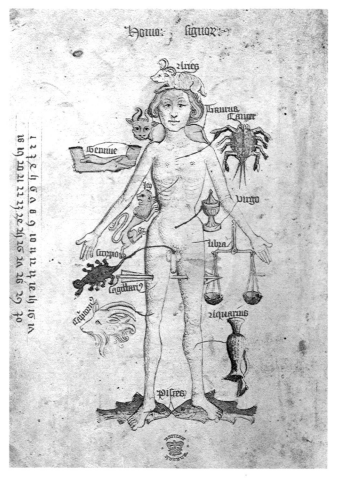

Nicholas Culpeper, the famous herbalist.

observed that the Moon hath great influence over plants ... and if it hath any such influence, then surely it is in the doubling of Flowers.'

But it was Master Nicholas Culpeper, who set up in Spitalfields as an Astrologer and Physician, who has most to say on the subject. His portrait, set in a double circle of the signs of the Zodiac and the medicinal plants which were his stock in trade, shows him to be a handsome young man, pictured above, the owner of Red Lion House, Spitalfields, a roomy country house in which he lived, studied and eventually died. 'I could not be ignorant, that as the cause is, so the cure must be,' he wrote in the Introduction to his *Herbal*, 'and therefore he that would know the reason of the Operation of the Herbs, must look up as high as the Stars, astrologically.' In his final *Instructions for the right use of the book*, he says:

And herein let me premise a word or two, The Herbs, Plants, etc., are now in the book appropriated to their proper planets. Therefore,

First, Consider what planet causeth the disease; that thou mayest find it in my aforesaid Judgment of Diseases.

Secondly, Consider what part of the body is afflicted

by the disease, and whether it lies in the flesh, or blood, or bones, or ventricles.

Thirdly, Consider by what planet the afflicted part of the body is governed: that my Judgment of Diseases will inform you also.

Fourthly, You may oppose diseases by Herbs of the planet, opposite to the planet that causes them as diseases of *Jupiter* by Herbs of *Mercury*, and the contrary; diseases of the *Luminaries* by the Herbs of *Saturn*, and the contrary; diseases of *Mars* by Herbs of *Venus*, and the contrary.

Fifthly, There is a way to cure diseases sometimes by *Sympathy*, and so every plant cures his own disease; as the *Sun* and the *Moon* by their Herbs cure the Eyes, *Saturn* the Spleen, *Jupiter* the Liver, *Mars* the Gall and diseases of choler, and *Venus* diseases in the Instruments of Generation.

William Coles wrote later, 'Though I admit not of Master Culpeper's Astrologicall way of every Planets Dominion over Plants, yet I conceive that the Sunne and Moon have generall influence upon them, the one for Heat and the other for Moisture; wherein the being of Plants consists.'

Even as late as 1826, Dr Parkins, at the conclusion of his *English Physician*, gives tables and instructions for 'Gathering Herbs and Plants in the Planetary Hour', and 'How to find the Planetary Hours for each Day in the Week', 'to such as study astrology, who are the only men I know that are fit to study physic, physic without astrology being like a lamp without oil.'

To this day the moon association persists. Extensive trials support some of the old customs. The old saying that vegetables yielding their crops above the soil should be planted on a waxing moon is confirmed, although the complementary one that plants yielding roots should be planted on a waning moon is only supported after September. Today's findings conclude that given the same moisture conditions, it is better to sow or plant during a waxing moon, preferably two days before the full moon, except after September, when it is best to sow or plant two days before the new moon.

Divination and dream plants

Where are you going? To Scarborough Fair.
Parsley, sage, rosemary, thyme,
Remember me to a bonny lass there,
For once she was a true lover of mine.

John Brand, *Popular Antiquities*, 1813

Here in this old folk song of *Scarborough Fair*, a mocking lover sends a message to his past love, listing the four divination plants that once brought them together. Each of the six following verses challenges her to do the impossible if she would regain his love.

Tell her to make me a cambric shirt,
Parsley, sage, rosemary, thyme,
Without any needle or thread worked in't,
And she shall be a true lover of mine.

Never did damsel receive a complete brush-off sent in so blithe and attractive a manner.

The orpine, *Sedum telephium*, with its handsome pinkish-purple flowers, was a popular divination plant. Lyte says in his translation of Rembert Dodoen's *Herbal* in 1578, 'The people of the country delight much to set it in pots and shelles on Midsummer even, or upon timber slattes, or trenchers daubed with clay, and so to set and hang it up in their houses, where it remaineth greene a long season, and groweth if it be sometimes oversprinkled with water.' It was a love charm known to the country girls as Midsummer Men, as its leaves bending to right or left would indicate the constancy or faithlessness of the loved one. On 22 January 1801, a small gold ring was found in a ploughed field near Cawood in Yorkshire, with a device of two orpine plants joined by a true-love knot with the motto, '*Ma fiance*

John Anstey Fitzgerald's 'Sleeping Beauty'.
There were many charms and spells which were meant to show
their future husbands to young girls in their dreams.

velt', 'My sweetheart wills', The stalks of the plants
were bent to each other, signifying the coming together in marriage. The ring was believed to be of the
fifteenth century.

Orpine is one of the divination plants recorded as
having been used by a young girl, but her name and
date is now forgotten. Having already made three
successful attempts by other methods the girl says, 'I
... stuck up two Midsummer Men, one for myself
and one for him. Now if his had died away, we
should never have come together, but I assure you
his blowed and turned to mine.' Appropriately, the
gentleman in question was a Mr Blossom. The re-
sourceful young diviner had already called upon the
assistance of hempseed. 'The same night [Mid-
summer Eve], exactly at 12 o'clock, I sowed
hempseed in our back-yard, and said to myself,
"Hemp-seed I sow, Hemp-seed I hoe, and he that is
my true-love come after me and mow." Will you
believe me? I looked back, and saw him behind me, as
plain as eyes could see him.' Hempseed with its
formula, could also be trusted to work on St

[67]

Valentine's day, but the day, and even the time, was as important as the method chosen. Here again our anonymous young woman is well informed on the subject so near her heart, though one would have thought that no further efforts on her part were needed. 'Our maid Betty tells me, that if I go backwards, without speaking a word, into the garden on Midsummer Eve, and gather a Rose, and keep it in a clean sheet of paper, without looking at it till Christmas Day, it will be as fresh as in June; and if I then stick it in my bosom, he that is to be my husband will come and take it out' – but could she wait until Christmas? Sadly we shall never know. Betty's love charm was well known in Devonshire, but there with the local variation that 'the young woman must be blindfolded, and that the charm must take place while the chimes are playing twelve', conditions set down in *The Literary Treasury of Science and Art*, 4 July 1835. Price 2d.

Another rose spell, under the title of *The Magic Rose*, appeared in *The Imperial Royal Fortune Teller*; anonymous, undated and 'Published in London by the Booksellers', thereby guarding against complaints by unsatisfied customers:

Gather your rose on the 27th of June, let it be full blown, and as bright a red as you can get; pluck it between the hours of three and four in the morning, taking care to have no witness of the transaction; convey it to your chamber, and hold it over a chafing-dish, or any convenient utensil for the purpose, in which there is charcoal and sulphur of brimstone; hold your rose over the smoke about four minutes, and you will see it have a wonderful effect on the flower. Before the rose gets the least cool, clap it in a sheet of writing paper, on which is written your own name and that of the young man you love best; also the date of the year, and the name of the morning-star that has the ascendancy at that time; fold it up, and seal it neatly with three separate seals, then run and bury the parcel at the foot of the tree from which you gathered the flower; and here let it remain untouched till the sixth of July, take it up at midnight, go to bed and place it under your pillow, and you will have a singular and most eventful dream before morning, or at least, before your usual time of rising. You may keep the rose under your head three nights without spoiling the charm; when you have done with the rose and paper, be sure to burn them.

Optimistic these young diviners may have been, credulous they certainly were, but illiterate they were not, and young men lived dangerously in those days.

The following spell must only be attempted on the eve of St Mary Magdalen's day, 22 July:

Let three young women assemble together on the eve of this saint in an upper apartment, where they are sure not to be disturbed, and let no one try whose age is more than 21, or it breaks the charm; get rum, wine, gin, vinegar, and water, and let each have a hand in preparing the potion. Put it in a ground glass vessel, no other will do; then let each young woman dip a sprig of rosemary in, and fasten it in her bosom, and taking three sips of the mixture get into bed; and the three must sleep together, but not a word must be spoken after the ceremony begins, and you will have true dreams, and of such a nature that you cannot possibly mistake your future destiny.

Morpheus, the god of sleep in classical mythology.

Let us hope that a cosy night was had by all.

It is tempting to quote more of these variations on the theme of love, from *The Imperial Royal Fortune Teller*, but there are other sources of Botonomancy, as it was called, and so only one more spell from this invaluable guide is included, for the charming picture it evokes. It is short and simple, and may be used, the book tells us, at any convenient time:

> Make a nosegay of various coloured flowers, one of a sort, a sprig of rue, and some yarrow off a grave, and bind all together with the hair from your head; sprinkle them with a few drops of oil of amber, using your left hand, and bind the flowers round your head when you retire to rest under your night-cap; put on clean sheets and linen, and your future fate will appear in your dream.

Ragged Robin, *Lychnis flos-cuculi*, Red Campion, *Melandrium rubrum*, Pennywort, *Umbilicus rupestris*, and Knapweed, *Centaurea nigra*, were all and indiscriminately considered charms for men only, since they shared the same popular name of Bachelor's Buttons. A plant was carried in the pocket, and their success or otherwise in love was judged by whether the plant thrived or not. Needless to say, by 1620 it was discovered that the girls had taken it over, and were carrying the plant under their aprons to entice the love of the owner.

Apples, garlic, poppy petals and vervain were all in use at one time or another, and in various places, and in *A Dialogue between Mistris Macquerella a suburb Bawd, Mrs. Scolopendra a noted Curtezan, and Mr. Pimpinello an Usher* (1650), Mistris Macquerella says, 'Some convenient, well situated Stall (wherein to sit and sell Thyme, Rue, and Rosemary, Apples, Garlike, and Saint Thomas Onyons) will be a fit place for me to practice Pennance in.' This introduces us for the first time to St Thomas's Onions, the strangest love divination yet, but its mention by Robert Burton in his *Anatomy of Melancholy* (1660), gives it a sort of respectability that Mistris Macquerella could not provide. Burton calls the custom *Cromnysmantia*, 'a kind of Divination with *Onions*, laid on the Altar at Christmas Eve, practised by Girls, to know they shall be married and how many husbands they shall have.'

In these same Dayes young wanton Gyrles, that meete for Marriage bee,
Doe search to know that Names of them that shall their husbandes bee.
Four Onyons, five, or eight, they take, and *make in every one*
Such names as they do fansie most, and best do think upon.
Then neere the chimney them they set and that same *onyon* then
That first doth sproute doth surely bear the name of their good man.

John Brand, *Popular Antiquities* , 1813

For a simple and solo divination with a St Thomas's onion, peel it and wrap it in a clean handkerchief, place it under the head (and presumably the pillow) and repeat the following lines:

Good St. Thomas, do me right,
And let my true-love come tonight,
. That I may see him in the face,
And him in my fond arms embrace.

Perhaps there may have been some advantage in collective divination?

A dream of fate is to be procured on the third day of the months between September and March by any odd number of young women not exceeding nine, if each of them strings nine acorns on a separate string (or as many acorns as there are young women), wraps them round a long stick of wood, and places it in the fire, precisely at midnight. The maidens, keeping perfect silence, must then sit round the fire till all the acorns are consumed, then take out the ashes, and retire to bed directly, repeating:

May love and marriage be the theme,
To visit me in this night's dream;
Gentle Venus, be my friend,
The image of my lover send;

[71]

Let me see his form and face,
And his occupation trace;
By a symbol or a sign,
Cupid, forward my design.

Collective divination was at times carried out with the most complicated ritual, and there is nothing to tell us whether it was achieved in the complete silence required, or perhaps, and rather more likely, with rustic giggles. Mugwort and plantain were always associated with midsummer, and it was believed that there could be found a rare coal under these plants for one hour in the day, and one day in the year. When John Aubrey was out walking at 12 o'clock on Midsummer Day, he relates how he saw about twenty-two young women, most of them well dressed and apparently all very busy weeding. They told him that they were looking for a coal under the root of a plantain to put beneath their heads that night, when they would be certain to dream about their future husbands.

In the northern counties of England, the plantain was used in a different manner. Two spikes, one for the girl and the other for the boy, were picked in full bloom, and all the tiny florets removed. The remaining kemps, as they were called, were wrapped in a dock leaf and laid under a stone. If the kemps have again blossomed when visited next morning, it will mean love between the two. John Clare, in his 'Shepherd's Calendar' (1827), describes a more romantic version:

Or, trying simple charms and spells,
Which rural superstition tells,
They pull the little blossom threads
From out the Knotweeds button heads,
And put the husk, with many a smile,
In their white bosoms for a while
Then, if they guess aright the swain,
Their love's sweet fancies try to gain,
'Tis said that ere it lies an hour,
'Twill blossom with a second flower,
And from the bosom's handkerchief
Bloom as it ne'er had lost a leaf.

The soul of a sleeper was supposed to wander away from his body and actually to visit the places, to see the persons and to perform the acts of which he dreams. In the past, dreams have been classified under the heading of Omens or Divination. Homer believed that dreams came from Jupiter, and the dreams of Homer were held in such esteem that they were known as golden dreams. Learned men wrote learned books on the interpretation of dreams, which caused a contributor to *The Gentleman's Magazine* for September 1751 to say that 'among the Grecians we find a whole Country using no other way for information, but going to sleep.' For those who dream about plants it became necessary, or so it was thought, to draw up a list of meanings, a sort of *Language of Dream Flowers*, based on past experience. There follow some of the results of these findings.

Almond
To dream of eating almonds means a journey. If they are sweet, it will be a prosperous one; if bitter, the reverse.

Apple
To dream of apples prophesies a long life, success in trade, and a lover's faithfulness.

Apricot
Dreaming of apricots denotes health, a speedy marriage, and every success in life.

Bean
To dream of any beans under any circumstances means trouble of some kind.

Box
To dream of box denotes long life and prosperity, also a happy marriage.

Bramble

An important plant in folklore. To dream of passing through places covered with brambles portends trouble; if they prick you, secret enemies will do you an injury; if they draw blood, expect heavy losses in trade; but to pass through brambles unhurt means triumph over enemies.

Cabbage

Cutting cabbage in dreams denotes jealousy on the part of wife, husband or lover. To dream of eating cabbage implies sickness for your loved ones, or loss of money.

Carrot

To dream of carrots signifies profit and strength to them that are at law for an inheritance.

Cherry

A dream of cherries denotes inconstancy and disappointments in life.

Clover

It is a happy augury to dream of clover, indicating health, prosperity and much happiness.

Corn

To dream you are gathering ripe corn promises success in your enterprises; if it is blighted or mildewed, you will be a considerable loser; if it is green, it will be a long time before you gain your purpose; if it becomes suddenly ripe, you will inherit unexpectedly. To dream you see a stack of corn burning signifies famine or death.

Cucumber

To dream of cucumbers denotes recovery to the invalid, and that you may then fall in love, or if you are in love already, that you will marry the one you love. It promises success in trade, and to a sailor, or a traveller, a pleasant voyage.

Currant

A dream of currants promises happiness in life, success in your undertakings, constancy in your sweetheart, and riches to a farmer or tradesman.

Cypress

To dream of a cypress tree foretells affliction and obstruction in business.

Daisy

It is lucky to dream of daisies in spring and summer, but unlucky in autumn.

Dandelion

A dream of dandelions brings misfortune, enemies and deceit on the part of loved ones.

Elderberry

To dream of elderberries denotes sickness.

Fig

A dream of figs promises wealth, prosperity and happiness, the realization of wishes, and a happy old age.

Filbert

It is a happy augury to dream of filberts – a sign of good health and happy old age, and everything that goes with it: success in love and marriage, and a numerous and prosperous family.

Fir tree

To dream you are in a forest of fir trees is a sign of suffering.

Garlic

If a man dreams of eating garlic, it signifies that he will discover hidden secrets, and meet with some domestic problems; yet to dream that he has garlic in the house is lucky.

Gooseberry

If a sailor dreams of gooseberries it indicates dangers in his next voyage. To a young girl it means an unfaithful husband.

Grass

To dream of grass is a good omen. If it is fresh and green, it will bring long life, good luck and great wealth. If withered, the sickness and possible death of loved ones. To dream of cutting grass portends great troubles.

Hazelnut

Discovering hazelnuts in dreams predicts the finding of treasure. To be cracking and eating them means riches, and content after toil.

Hyssop

A dream of hyssop means that friends will bring you peace and happiness.

Ivy

It is considered extremely lucky to dream of ivy, bringing friendship, happiness and good fortune, honour and success to the dreamer.

Jasmine

It is lucky, especially to lovers, to dream of jasmine.

Lettuce

To dream of eating a lettuce salad is believed to forecast trouble and difficulty in the management of affairs.

Lily

Dreaming of lilies in bloom foretells marriage, happiness and prosperity. Lilies out of season or withered signify frustration of hopes, and the death or severe illness of someone you love.

Marigold

Prosperity, success and a happy marriage may follow a dream of marigolds.

Melon

A young woman who dreams of melons will marry a rich foreigner and live with him in a foreign land. A young man dreaming of melons will marry a rich foreign lady, by whom he will have a large family, but they will die young. If a sick person dreams of melons, their juicy flesh promises recovery.

Mushroom

Dream oracles state that mushrooms prophesy fleeting happiness; and that to dream of picking them indicates a lack of attachment on the part of lover or married partner.

Myrtle

To dream of myrtle promises many lovers and a legacy. If a married person dreams of myrtle it foretells a second marriage. A similar dream for a second time denotes a second marriage to a person who has also been married before.

Nettle

In dream lore, to be stung by nettles indicates vexation and disappointment. Gathering nettles means that someone has formed a favourable opinion of you; and if the dreamer is married, then family life will be harmonious.

Nutmeg

A dream of nutmegs is a sign of many impending changes.

Oak tree

To dream of a green oak signifies a long and happy life; a withered oak foretells poverty in old age. Thriving oaks promise male children who will win distinction. Oaks bearing acorns mean wealth, and a blasted oak, death.

Onions

> To dream of eating onions means
> Much strife in thy domestic scenes;
> Secrets found out or else betrayed,
> And many falsehoods made and said.

T. F. Thistleton Dyer, *The Folklore of Plants*

Orange

Dream books hint darkly that at all times a dream of oranges is a very unfavourable omen.

Palm

To dream of a palm tree is a very good omen, particularly if it is in full bloom, when it predicts success and good fortune.

Peach

A dream of peaches is a sign of content, health and pleasure.

Pear

Dreaming of ripe pears promises riches and happiness; if unripe, adversity; if baked, great success in business; to a woman a dream of pears means that she will marry above her rank.

Pine

According to this ancient and devastating tradition, the pine tree seen in a dream foretells dissolution.

Plum

To dream of plums is a warning of ill-health, losses, infidelity and much vexation in the married state.

Pomegranate

A dream of pomegranates means good fortune and success. To the lover, a faithful and accomplished sweetheart; to the married, wealth, children and success in business.

Quince

To dream of quinces promises speedy release from troubles and sickness.

Raspberry

Dreaming of raspberries will bring success and happiness in marriage, fidelity in a sweetheart and good news from abroad.

Rose

Nothing can be happier than a dream of roses. To the lover, a happy marriage. To the farmer and sailor, prosperity and ultimate independence. Withered roses, however, mean decay of fortune and disappointment.

Sycamore

To dream of a sycamore tree foretells jealousy to the married. It promises marriage to the unmarried.

Thistle

To dream about being surrounded by thistle is a lucky omen, promising pleasant events shortly.

Turnip

A dream of turnips denotes fruitless toil.

Vine

Dreaming of vines denotes health, prosperity and fertility, for which, says a dream oracle, 'we have the example of Astyages, King of the Medes, who dreamed that his daughter brought forth a Vine, which was a prognostic of the grandeur, riches and felicity of the great Cyrus, who was born of her after this dream.'

Violet

To dream of violets is a promise of advancement in life.

Wallflower

Dreams of wallflowers foretell to a lover that his sweetheart is faithful; to an invalid that recovery will shortly follow; and to a woman who dreams that she is picking the flowers for a bouquet, that the worthiest of her admirers has yet to propose to her.

Willow

With the strange inconsistency of dreams, if the dreamer is mourning under a willow over some calamity, it is a happy omen, bringing good news.

Wormwood

A dream plant of good omen.

Yarrow

To dream of picking yarrow for medicinal purposes means that the dreamer will shortly have some good news.

Perhaps, after all this wishful dreaming, it is refreshing to learn that there is a recipe to prevent dreaming: 'Take vervain and hang it about a man's neck, and let him drink some of the juice before going to bed; certainly he will not dream if he does so.' To dream, or not to dream – that is the question.

Angels, devils and witches

Looking at the strangely shaped and delicately coloured petals of many of our wild flowers, it is odd to
find that devil names are far more frequently bestowed on them than angel names. A few flowers
may even be known as angel in one part of the
country and devil in another. Germander Speedwell,
Veronica chamaedrys, for instance, is very suitably
known as Angel's Eyes in Devon and Somerset, but
as Devil's Eyes in Warwickshire, as well as Deil's
(Devil's) Flower in Scotland. Can its association
with the devil be because of its persistent appearance
in the lawn, where it is least appreciated; or how
otherwise can those wide blue eyes have been so
misappropriated?

Angels-and-Devils is one of the less scurrilous
names given to Cuckoo Pint, *Arum maculatum*, with
as a variant, Devil's Men or Devil's Ladies and
Gentlemen. This may be a long-forgotten reference

Deadly nightshade (*Atropa belladonna*), one of many plants
attributed to witchcraft and the Devil.

A young witch prepares a love charm, from a
fifteenth-century Flemish painting.

OPPOSITE ABOVE:
The poppy, from *Les Fleurs Animées* of 1857.

OPPOSITE BELOW:
The ash tree (on the left) traditionally provided
the wood for witches' broomsticks.

to the form of the spadix and the spathe, which stood for copulation in early beliefs. The wickedly poisonous thorn apple, *Datura stramonium*, has avoided the devil's grasp, and is known in the rare country districts in which it is to be found as Angel's Trumpets, in acknowledgement of its beautiful flowers. That most handsome, healing and holy of plants called angelica, *Angelica sylvestris*, brings the list of angel flowers to an end, with the exception of ribwort, *Plantago lanceolata*, which long ago suggested the children's game of 'fighting cocks', and gave rise to the popular name of Devils-and-Angels.

Poisonous properties, unpleasant smells and strangling roots have all resulted in Devil, Deil or Old Man names. Deadly nightshade, *Atropa belladonna*, which Gerard called a 'plant so furious and deadly', was known in various parts of the country as Devil's Rhubarb, Cherries or Berries. Not only has stinking mayweed, *Anthemis cotula*, been conscripted to the devil's tribe, but ragwort, *Senecio jacobaea*, which as well as possessing a rank smell acts as a host to the crawling masses of the striped caterpillars of the cinnabar moths, and is therefore doubly unpleasant, is known as Devildums. Perhaps it is a little hard on the feverfew, *Chrysanthemum parthenium*, and the oxe-eye daisy, *Chrysanthemum leucanthemum*, both useful physic plants, to be called Devil Daisies, just because they are possessors of a good pungent country smell. Old Reekie himself has a talent for the unpleasant, and the nettle, *Urtica dioica*, is suitably known as the Devil's Plaything, for the painful sting inflicted by its leaves. That beautiful little white bouquet-flower ramsons, *Allium ursinum*, which startles us at first meeting by the strong whiffs of garlic it exudes, is known as Devil-may-care; and fool's parsley, *Aethusa cynapium*, the plant which Gerard accused of being little but 'a naughtie smell', is Devil's Wand.

Farming families are probably responsible for naming most of the field pests with their smothering roots: the broomrape, the bindweeds and the dodder, which they say is spun by the devil nightly to destroy the crops – all are dedicated to the old man. The hated but lovely field poppies, *Papaver rhoea*, are seldom seen in our fields today, for the farmers have won that particular battle, but their name of Devil's Tongue still echoes.

Witches had a more personal contact with suffering humanity than did the devil, who works his evil at one remove. Only the length of a broomstick divides the devil from his handmaidens, the witches. They were learned in plant lore, and to a witch a garden was as vital as her cauldron and her familiar, an imp in the shape of a cat, or perhaps a bat, mole, owl or toad. Almost as important, she needed some straggly hawthorns to hedge round her patch of earth, to shield her from prying eyes. 'Hedge' is derived from the same word as 'hag', and hags or witches were believed to shelter in hedges, particularly hawthorn hedges; indeed, hags, hedges and hawthorn are closely associated. The sun never shone on a witch's garden, for the least gleam would have ruined the magical properties of her herbs. There she grew enchanter's nightshade, known also as *Circaea lutetiana*, after Circe, a sorceress celebrated for her knowledge of venomous herbs. Without this small and inconspicuous plant, a witch would be quite incapable of raising the devil and her incantations would be unavailing. In 1869, when witchcraft was little but a retreating shadow over the land, Robert Tyas wrote, 'In damp and humid places, where the superstitious mind may imagine every kind of hideous reptile, and birds of evil omen to congregate; and plants and weeds of noxious properties to thrive; and where the wizened wizard and the shrivelled hag, of face repulsive, might most fitly perform their incantations; there does this plant delight to grow, as "amid the mouldering bones and decayed coffins in the ruinous vaults of Sleaford church, in Lincolnshire", and like localities.'

In a corner of her garden would be her cracked and skinny yew tree, *Taxus bacata*, the ground beneath parched and bare, for it is a well-known fact that nothing will grow beneath a yew. However, a few 'slips of yew sliver'd in the moon's eclipse' would never come amiss in her spells. The wood of a yew tree is unsuitable for broomsticks, so she would have to depend on a nearby ash, a branch of which used for a broom-handle would protect her from drowning. How vital the ash tree, *Fraxinus excelsior*, could be, only a witch would know, for any poor skinny old hag might be thrown into deep water to prove her innocence. Her hands and feet would be tied together crosswise, the thumb of the right hand to the big toe of the left foot, and vice versa. Then, wrapped in a blanket, or sometimes in her birthday suit, she would be tossed into a river or a pond. Let her prove she isn't a witch by swimming to the other side, people said. If she floated, she had to be a witch, and would be suitably dealt with. If she drowned, her character would be cleared. In spite of this and ever hopeful, she chose ash-wood for her broom-handle, and a bunch of birch twigs, tied with osiers, *Salix viminalis*, for her broom. Osiers were Hecate's plants, and Hecate presided over the infernal regions, therefore osiers were a protection for witches, sorely needed in a precarious existence.

In what served as the herbaceous border in her ill-kempt garden, she would grow wormwood, which had sprung up in the track of the serpent when it was driven out of Eden. Monkshood, better known to witches as wolfbane, whose venom came from the foam that dripped from the fangs of the three-headed dog Cerberus, would be sure to flourish there. She would also grow hemlock, *Conium maculatum*, for 'root of hemlock digg'd i' the dark' was always useful. Did she not say in Ben Jonson's *Masque of Queens* (*c.*1605):

> And I ha' been plucking plants among
> Hemlock, Henbane, Adder's Tongue;
> Nightshade, Moonwort, Libbard's bane,
> And twice by the dogs had like to be ta'en.

The horned poppy, *Glaucium flavum*, another incantation plant, was desirable but rather hard to come by, since it grows only by the sea, but Jonson included it in the *Witches' Song*:

> Yes, I have brought to help our vows,
> Horned poppy, Cypress bough,
> The fig tree wild that grows on tombs,
> And juice which from the larch tree comes.

Outside her garden, in fields and ditches, she would go hunting for other herbs: foxgloves, *Digitalis purpurea*, or witch's bells to decorate her skinny fingers; mullein, *Verbascum thapsus*, or hag taper for her candles; harebells, *Campanula rotundifolia*, for thimbles, and ragwort, *Senecio*, which had the useful property of turning into a horse, so that she could fly over the countryside when a broomstick was not at hand. Even a bundle of hay would serve her for Pegasus. No one ever saw the black witch picking her herbs, for they had to be harvested in secret, at certain phases of the moon and seasons of the year, and the signs of the Zodiac had to be consulted. Francis Bacon, early in the seventeenth century, wrote that 'the Ointment of Witches ... is reported to be made of the Fat of Children digged out of their Graves; of the juices of Smallage, Wolf-Bane, and Cinque-Foil, mingled with the meal of fine Wheat: but I suppose the soporiferous medicines are likest to do it, which are Hen-bane, Hemlock, Mandrake, Moon-shade, or rather Night-shade, Tobacco, Opium, Saffron, Poplar-leaves, etc.'

But life wasn't all witches' sabbaths, curses and covens. There were grey witches also who, like other grey people, left no story behind them. They cured when they chose, and they attempted to kill if anyone made it worth their while. Since their results were seldom dramatic and their identities obscure, they usually kept out of the duck-pond, and the trial by torture that might have followed, but for that reason we know little about them. There were also white witches, who knew as many healing herbs and

A sixteenth-century view of the Devil carrying a witch off to Hell.

traditional rites and ceremonies as the others, but preferred to earn a humble reputation in their village for the making of love charms and the soothing of sick babies. They prevented horses from being hag-ridden, and knew how to protect a house from lightning, and were often consulted in the finding of lost property and the seeking-out of thieves. The detection of black witches by white witches, however, was ill-advised. They did good with their potions, and were kindly enough – or perhaps timid enough – to avoid such plants as hemlock and henbane and others of a poisonous nature, and sought no such publicity as night-riding on broomsticks to attend Witches' Sabbats, nor midnight dancing on the heath. They were not only permitted to live in peace with their fellows, but probably even rose to a position of some eminence in rural society, by doing a modest trade in raising fair winds for sailors, and bringing rain to the crops, and helping barren women to conceive; as well as giving valuable service as the village midwife should their efforts have proved successful.

The ivy that grew in the white witch's garden was needed for the divination of sickness, as we may see in the following extract from Lupton's *Tenth Book of Notable Things* (1660) which says:

[88]

A witches' sabbath.

Lay a green Ivie-Leafe in a Dish, or other Vessel of Fair Water, either for yourselfe or for any other, on New-Year's Even at Night, and cover the Water in the said Vessel, and set it in a sure or safe place, until Twelfe Even nexte after, (which will be the 5th day of January,) and then take the said Ivie-Leafe out of the said Water, and mark well if the said Leafe be fair and green as it was before, for then you, or the party for whome you lay it into the Water, will be whole and sound, and safe from any sicknesse all the next yeare following. But if you find any black spots thereon, then you, or the parties for whom you laid it into the Water, will be sicke the same yeare following. And if the spots be on the upper part of the Leafe toward the Stalke, then the sicknesse or paine will be in the Head, or in the Neck, or thereabout. And if it be spotted nigh the midst of the Leafe, then the sicknesse will be about the Stomach or Heart. And likewise judge, that the disease or grief will be in that part of the body, according as you see the black spots in the nether or sharp end of the Leafe to signifie the paines or diseases in the Feet. And if the Leafe bee spotted all over, then it signifies that you, or the partie, shall dye that yeare following. You may prove this for many or few, at one time, by putting them in Water, for everie one a Leafe of green Ivie (so that everie Leafe be dated or marked to whom it doth belong). This was credibly told to me to be very certain.

But above all, white witches were expected to supply the boys and girls – especially the girls – with love philtres. These might include vervain, which secures affection from those who give it to those who take it; the seed of endive, which enables a lover to inspire his lass with a belief that he possesses all the good qualities that she could wish for; and the root of the male fern. This song,

> 'Twas the maiden's matchless beauty
>   That drew my heart a-nigh;
> Not the fern-root potion,
>   But the glance of her blue eye,

suggests that there were times when the assistance of fern root might have been considered.

Then there was cumin seed, to inspire attachment, especially useful to give to soldiers and sailors, who were notably easy to catch but hard to hold; cyclamen excited love and desire, so it was worth a try. Basil, dear to women and to lovers, is also dedicated to Satan, and behaves in a thoroughly unpredictable manner. Francis Bacon states that 'if Basil is exposed too much to the sun, it changes into Wild Thyme', so it might be more satisfactory to use periwinkle, which ensures lasting affection between man and woman. There were others too that the witch might prescribe, if you crossed her palm with silver. She might even give a girl a clover-leaf to put in her lover's shoe, so that he would be faithful during his absence.

Village folk who refused to put their trust in witches of any shade grew a number of anti-witch plants for their own protection, the most valuable of all being *Herba benedicta*, since it was well known that when a root of herb bennet is in the house the devil is powerless, for it is blessed above all others. Even today its trefoil leaf and five golden petals, signifying Christ's five wounds, may be recognized in cathedral and church architecture.

Those that could read might seek information from the herbals. William Coles had useful advice to offer. He said that '*Herba paris* takes away Evill done by Witchcraft', and affirms that he knew it to be true by experience. Also that 'if one hang Mistletoe about their neck, the Witches can have no power of him. The roots of Anglica [angelica] do likewise availe much in the same case, if a man carry them about him.'

Reginald Scot had already, in 1584, noted that:

> To be delivered from Witches they hang in their Entries an Herb called Pentaphyllon [Cinquefoil], also an Olive Branch: also Frankincense, Myrrh, Valerian, Verven, Palm, Antirchmon, etc., also Haythorn, otherwise Whitethorn gathered on May Day ... in some countries ... they hang Scilla, (which is either a root, or rather in this place, garlicke,) in the roof of the House, to keep away Witches and Spirits;

and so they do Alicium [Alyssum] also . . . the House where *Herba betonica* is sown, is free from all mischiefs.

Pennyroyal could be used in broth to cause people to 'see double', and milkmaids preferred a churnstaff of rowan wood, since it saved the butter, particularly if she had already beaten the cow with a rowan twig. Herd-boys drove the cattle with a rowan twig – no great difficulty, since it usually grew at the farm door. If the floors were regularly rubbed with rue, no witch could enter, and men might be preserved from witchcraft by green leaves consecrated on Palm Sunday. According to an old manuscript in Chetham Library, Manchester, pimpernel was also reliable as an anti-witch plant, 'as Mother Bumby doth affirm', and this good lady has left other such advice to be handed down to posterity.

Gradually, early in the eighteenth century, witchcraft and anti-witchcraft, and the cruelty and hatred that they had engendered, drew to an end. Witches, with their spells and cauldrons, passed into legend and thence into the comfortably frightening story-books that children still enjoy today, although in ever decreasing numbers. In 1736, by Act of Parliament, it was laid down that 'no Prosecution, Suit, or Proceedings, shall be commenced or carried on against any Person or Persons for Witchcraft, Sorcery, Inchantment, or Conjuration, or for charging another with any such Offence in any Court whatsoever in Great Britain.' It took a long time for broomsticks to give way to spaceships, but the skies have been cleared of cobwebs, and the earth of the persecution of harmless old women.

The saddest thing in the history of witches and witch-hunts must remain that when a miserable old hag was caught and tried, and almost inevitably found guilty, her witchcraft was of no avail. Her magic herbs failed her in her hour of need, and she was hanged or burnt, and buried in unhallowed ground, an aspen laid above her to prevent her ever again from riding abroad.

The origins of the language and sentiment of flowers

That flowers were given meanings and characteristics of their own by the ancient Greeks and Romans can hardly seem surprising when we read the legends of their slain gods and frightened nymphs and their inevitable metamorphosis into flowers. Hyacinthus killed by a quoit, Narcissus drowning in his own watery image, Daphne fleeing from Apollo: each has left us a flower or plant to perpetuate their names. The hyacinth and narcissus can now be purchased in and sometimes out of season at any supermarket, and we may drive to a nursery at the weekend and choose for ourselves a well-shaped daphne bush or laurel as a direct inheritance from the gods, although there will be no mention of this on the neat little label on the plant. It is believed that the Greeks understood the art of sending messages by a bouquet, and it is evident from the *Dream Book of Artimedorus*, who lived about AD 170, that every flower of which their garlands were composed had a particular meaning, although we have no certain knowledge of this ancient flower language. The Chinese, whose chronicles antedate the historic records of all other nations, used a simple but complete mode of communication by means of florigraphic signs. The Assyrians, Egyptians and Indians also used floral symbols.

In England during the reign of Elizabeth I, we get hints of what is to come, in a verse believed to be by William Hunnis, which must be one of our earliest mentions of a means of communication by flowers. Here we have verses beginning, 'Gilly-flowers is for gentleness, Which in me shall remain', and 'Marigolds is for marriage, That would our minds suffice', or 'Cowslips is for counsel, For secrets us between'. There are others (see Lavender and Violet below), which will appear later, and all of them turn up again 300 years on, when what might be described as Flower-Linguamania seized the Victorian imagination. Meanwhile, religious flower symbolism was never forgotten, and between 1609 and 1633, a flower carol was being sung in Flanders, later known to us as *King Jesus Hath a Garden*. This joyous carol that we still sing each Christmastide, makes use of the old familiar flowers in a similar symbolic way:

> The Lily, white in blossom there, is Chastity;
> The Violet, with sweet perfume, Humility.
>> There naught is heard
>> But Paradise bird,
>>> Harp, dulcimer, lute,
>> With cymbal,
>> Trump and tymbal,
>>> And the tender soothing flute.

The next verse introduces two more flowers with their virtues:

> The bonny Damask-rose is known as Patience;
> The blith and thrifty Marigold, Obedience,

and so on. It seems that flowers have always meant more than their beauty and perfume.

On 16 March 1718, Lady Mary Wortley-Montague wrote from Constantinople to a friend, giving her an enthusiastic description of a secret message of love that might be conveyed by such objects as a pearl, a clove, etc., enclosed in a small purse, each having an agreed meaning. Aubrey de la Mottraie, who introduced the first flower language into France, wrote, 'Fruit, Flowers, and Gold and Silver Thread or silk of divers Colours . . . have each of them their particular meaning explain'd by certain Turkish verses, which young Girls learn by Tradition of one another.' La Mottraie was the companion of Charles XII, King of Sweden, who invaded Denmark in 1700 and defeated the Russians at Narva in the same year. He was in turn defeated by Peter the Great in 1709. Charles escaped into Turkey, and it is likely that he and La Mottraie learnt there the Turkish secret love language from which Aimé Martin evolved the French version. Martin's *Langage des Fleurs* was first published in 1830, and he also produced a similar version with different illustrations under the pseudonym of Madame Charlotte de la Tour. This was translated into the *Blumen-Sprache* of Germany, and thence found its way, no doubt on the wings of Cupid, to many other parts of the world.

By 1847, a certain Thomas Miller, having for guide as he claims 'no less authorities than Chaucer, Spenser, Shakespeare and Milton', published a little book which he dedicated to 'The Rosebud of England, The Princess Royal', entitled *The Poetical Language of Flowers; or, The Pilgrimage of Love*. About the time of Miller's death in 1874, no less a writer than Captain Marryat, author of *Peter Simple, Midshipman Easy*, and other classic sea stories, must have been working on his own completely original method of communication by flowers. This he called *The Floral Telegraph or Affection's Signals*, and it was a most sophisticated version of a hitherto artless means of correspondence. The vocabulary contains emblems that would take the reader to The English Opera, Covent Garden Theatre and The British Museum, with equal readiness, and for those with fewer cultural pretensions, The Fancy Fair or Greenwich Park. The flowers are tied together on a knotted cord of ribbon, and when this is unrolled, the initiated may read quite complicated messages, in which the knots, as well as the flowers, have significance. In no other Language of Flowers still in existence can such vital messages be conveyed as in Vocabulary 3, no. 289, 'I cannot play Juliet to your Romeo'; no. 295, 'I shall be watching for your approach'; or no. 369, a brief but irrevocable *cri de coeur*, 'Brighton'.

Now small and gilt-edged flower language booklets appeared in every bookshop. One such claimed that 'The oracle cannot fail to excite much harmless mirth; but some kinds of floral divinations, as these pages testify, have oft produced deeper thoughts and more serious consequences,' as they probably did. Inevitably came *The Bible Language of Flowers*, and *Floral Birthday Books*, birthday cards, valentines, and flower pieces to be prettily tinkled on the piano and as prettily left lying about, to display their evocative covers, followed.

On into the Edwardian era the floral communications swept, and picture postcards carrying abridged versions of the flower language, or with shiny photographs of lovers in less than compromising positions against a background of 'Lilac, First Emotions of Love,' or 'Sainfoin, Agitation', gladdened the hearts of the postmen as well as the recipients. During this period, as if flowers were not enough, even the angle at which the postage stamp was applied carried a secret message; a new and ingenious code with which, it was hoped, neither postman nor parent would be *au fait*. That is, until yet another postcard was issued displaying the Language of Stamps, in all its subtlety, and the game was up.

One more variation on the theme of Love, was the publication of the first, and perhaps the only book explaining the origins of *The Language and Sentiments of Flowers*. It was written by Arthur Freeling and published in 1857, under the title of *Flowers, Their Use and Beauty, Language and Sentiment*. Arthur Freeling, while accepting the usual vocabulary, must have done considerable research on the reasons why, for instance, an evening primrose has Inconstancy and Uncertainty as its sentiment; or why Submission was chosen as the emblem of grasses. A condensed and updated version of this well-intentioned work is now offered to collectors of these little books, and to lovers who have experienced the difficulties, or perhaps the unwisdom, of setting pen to paper, and would prefer to Say it with Flowers.

Amaranth   *Immortality*

The ancients placed wreaths of amaranth on the brows of their gods. At the funeral rites of Achilles, the Thessalians wore crowns of amaranth in honour of the dead hero. Queen Christina of Sweden, renouncing her throne with a view to obtaining immortality by devoting herself to a life of letters, founded the order of 'The Knights of the Amaranth' to immortalize the sacrifice. Milton placed it on the bowers of Paradise, 'Fast by the tree of life'.

Anemone *Anticipation*

The appearance of the anemone heralds the approach of spring and, where blooming amid the snow, promises that the reign of Boreas is nearly over, and that his white mantle will soon be withdrawn.

Auricula *Pride*

The richness of the many colours of the auricula, its velvety texture, and the white 'meal' with which many of its flowers are powdered, have caused it to be made the symbol of Pride in the Language of Flowers.

Bay *I change but in dying*

The sweet bay tree is an evergreen, and since the leaves change only in death it has been chosen as the emblem of unchanging affection.

Box *Stoicism*

The plant is changed neither by cold nor by heat. It is said to prefer the shade, but lives in sunshine, unimpressed by either, and thus it lives on unaffected by storm or sun, to a great age.

Broom *Ardour*

The broom was chosen as the emblem of ardour from the fact that its intensely bright yellow flowers remind us of the warmth of feeling or the ardour of love.

Buttercup and Kingcup *Riches*

These flowers foretell future wealth to anyone on whom they reflect a vivid gold when the flower is

OPPOSITE ABOVE:
'The language of
Flowers' by G. D. Leslie,
1885.

OPPOSITE BELOW:
'Broken Vows' by
Philip Calderon.

RIGHT:
Wych elm (wych hazel)
by B. Wilkes from *The
English Moths and
Butterflies*.

BELOW:
Primrose seller from
'Cries of London'. A
colour engraving after
F. Wheatley, 1793.

held near to the face. The poet Southey referred to this belief: 'Bright flowering kingcups promise future wealth.'

Camellia   *Unpretending excellence*

The excellence of this large and beautiful rose-like flower, lies in it also being an evergreen with splendid glossy leaves.

> The chaste camellia's pure and spotless bloom,
> That boasts no fragrance and conceals no thorn.

Cardinal flower   *Distinction*

Otherwise known as *Lobelia cardinalis*, this brilliantly scarlet flower, 'Lobelia, attired like a queen in her pride', can scarcely avoid notice.

Carnation   *Pure love*

The carnation, either dark red or white, has become by cultivation doubled, striped, flaked or marbled, but it shows a tendency to return to its original simplicity. Like pure love it shows a desire for constancy.

Carolina allspice   *Benevolence*

The warm aromatic flavour of this plant may have suggested it as an emblem of benevolence. It has, however, a further claim, for if the terminal leaf-buds are removed, a succession of flowers may be obtained, each bud being followed by two flowers: a certain indication of the plant's benevolence.

Cedar   *Incorruptibility*

The cedar was believed by the ancients not only to be incorruptible, but also to preserve all things free from corruption that were enclosed in its wood. The Egyptians used the gum exuded from the trunk in embalming their mummies. Valuable books were kept in cedar boxes to guard them from the destructive book-worm and today entomologists keep their specimens in cedar-lined cases.

The Chaste tree   *Apathy. To live without love*

The priestesses of Ceres slept upon couches covered

with the leaves of this tree, *Vitex agnus castus*, to subdue their feelings of sensuality. Christian nuns used to drink a decoction of the leaves to calm unhallowed emotions. Certainly a suitable emblem for those fated to live without love.

Clover *Happiness*

To find a four-leaved white clover, which is the true shamrock, is even today regarded as a lucky omen. The three-leaved shamrock is the national emblem of Ireland. He that finds a four-leaved shamrock will find happiness, they say, since both being rare, folk are as likely to find the one as the other.

Crocus *Youthful gladness*

These bright heralds of spring, so soon departed, have been made fitting symbols of the happiness of youth.

Daffodil *Regret*

One of the most cheerful sights of spring is 'a host of golden daffodils', or even just one daffodil; and yet, because the flower droops its head, it is doomed. Even the usually cheerful Herrick says:

> When a daffadil I see
> Hanging down her head t'ward me,
> Guess I may, what I must be;
> First, I shall decline my head,
> Secondly I shall be dead,
> Lastly, safely buried.

Daisy *Innocence*

Pliny regarded the daisy as useless. 'These be flowers of the meadows, and most of such are of no use at all.' 'No use at all,' agreed Walter de la Mare, 'Except only to make a skylark of every heart whose owner has eyes in his head for a daisy's simple looks, its marvellous making, and the sheer happiness of their multitudes wide open in the sun and adrowse in the evening twilight.' Daisies have been, and always will be the symbol of childhood and innocence.

Dandelion *Oracle*

Once the shepherds', the schoolboys' and the lovers'

oracle, the dandelion prophesied the weather by the opening and closing of its flowers. Dandelion clocks told not only the time, but whether one's lover was false or true, by the number of puffs of breath needed to rid it of its thistledown. What flower more suitable to be consulted as an oracle?

Eglantine or Sweet briar   *Simplicity*

We are told that a wreath of eglantine or sweet briar was the prize offered to victorious poets at the Floral Games in Greece. One can only think that the honour was in the winning and not in the wearing of this emblem of simplicity.

Evening primrose   *Inconstancy, uncertainty*

This flower has the strange reputation of being repeatedly lost and found in gardens, without the owners being able to account for its appearance and disappearance. Hence its meaning of inconstancy and uncertainty is well deserved.

Forget-me-not   *True love*

The origin of the sentiment attached to this flower is as simple as the flower itself – true love can never be forgotten.

Geranium   *Comfort*

Because of the strangely refreshing perfume of the geranium, it has been made the symbol of comfort, a sort of floral smelling-salts.

Globe amaranth   *Unchangeableness*

We are told that we must look to the globe amaranth itself for the origin of this sentiment, as its flowers retain their beauty for several years, and are in constant use for the *imortelles* which once decorated the graves of the departed. Now their place has been taken by the even more unchangeable plastic.

Grasses   *Submission*

The nations of the west, according to Herodotus,

used grass as a sign of submission. When William the Conqueror landed at Pevensey, one of his followers laid hold of the thatch of a cottage, and presented a piece of it to William as a 'seizin' or acknowledgement that the kingdom accepted his rule and submitted to it.

Harebell   *Grief*

The drooping head of this delicate flower makes it a fit emblem for the sentiment of grief.

> The Harebell, as with grief depress'd,
>   Bowing her fragrance.
>
> Anon.

Hawthorn   *Hope*

The altar of Hymen was lit by torches of hawthorn, a symbol of present happiness and future hope. Youthful Athenian maidens carried hawthorn branches at the wedddings of their friends, just as bridesmaids carry flowers today.

Holly   *Domestic happiness*

Prickles or no, there is something warm and comfortable about the holly – conjuring up visions of yule logs, cards on the mantelpiece and robins at the door.

Hollyhock   *Ambition*

From its numerous flowers, the hollyhock has often been the emblem of fecundity, but its desire to rise above most other garden plants has made it also symbolic of ambition.

Honeysuckle   *Fidelity*

Anyone who has tried to remove a honeysuckle from its support will agree that never could there be a more suitable and tenacious emblem of fidelity.

Hyacinth   *Sorrow*

When Apollo and Hyacinth were playing at quoits upon the banks of the river, Hyacinth was struck on the temple with one of the quoits and killed. Apollo, unable to restore him to life, asked the gods to change the boy into the flower that has since borne his name, and it remains the emblem of Apollo's sorrow.

Ivy   *Wedded love*

Owing to the unchangeable green of its leaves, the ivy was used by the Greeks to decorate the altar of Hymen, as a suitable symbol of wedded love.

Jasmine   *Amiability*

When in the darkness of the night, other flowers cannot be seen, and withhold their perfume for another day, the amiable white jasmine confers upon us its sweetest fragrance.

Larkspur   *Lightness*

In the past this flower was known as lark's head, lark's toes, lark's claw and finally, larkspur, from its resemblance to a bird so light that it can soar above our heads until it is a mere speck in the blue. It has thus been given as the emblem of lightness.

Lavender   *Acknowledgement of love*

Lavender was an Elizabethan lover's flower.

> Lavender is for lovers true,
> Which evermore be fain,
> Desiring always for to have
> Some pleasure for their pain.
>
> Elizabethan Lyric

Lilac   *The first emotions of love*

It is said that the great botanical artist Spaendonck threw down his pencil in despair, when trying to paint the variety and beauty of each tiny floret of the lilac, and as delicate and variable as this flower, are the first emotions of love.

Lily of the valley   *Return of happiness*

Legend tells of the love of a lily of the valley for a

nightingale, and how the bird would not return to the wood until the flower bloomed each May. This story is the origin of its meaning in the Language of Flowers.

Love lies bleeding *Desertion*

A flower with such a name cannot be omitted from the Language of Flowers: its sentiment is all too clear.

Lupin *Dejection*

Another sad emblem, the lupin folds its drooping leaves at the setting of the sun, as if mourning the absence of the god of day.

Mignonette *Your qualities surpass your charms*

Since the unfortunate mignonette is valued rather for its scent than its beauty, it has been cursed with a sentiment that would seem a doubtful compliment to either young woman or flower.

Mimosa *Sensitivity*

The mimosa is otherwise known as the Sensitive Plant, since not only does it shrink from the human touch, but if a cloud passes over it, it will similarly react. It might have been made the symbol of the Victorian young lady.

Myrtle *Love*

It is an Arabian tradition that when Adam was driven from Paradise, he carried in his hand a sprig of myrtle from the bower in which he first declared his love to Eve.

Nightshade *Truth*

Truth, we are told, lived at the bottom of a well. She was, as she needed to be, of divine origin, and in dispensing her blessings always mixed them with more or less bitterness. Because both plant and emblem choose to live in the shade, the nightshade was given truth as an emblem.

Olive   *Peace*

When the Dove returned to the Ark carrying an olive branch in its beak the olive was made the emblem of Peace, since the waters were retiring from the earth and the anger of the Lord had ceased.

Orange flower   *Chastity*

Jupiter gave Juno an orange at their marriage, and young brides have been wearing orange blossom ever since. Perhaps it was over-anxious mamas that caused the flower to be made the emblem of Chastity.

Pansy, heartsease   *Tender and pleasant thoughts*

Shakespeare is the authority for this sentiment. In the words of his gentle Ophelia, 'I pray you, love, remember, there is Pansies – that's for thoughts.'

Passion flower   *Religious fervour*

In their religious zeal, the Spanish settlers in South America saw in the Maracoc, as it was then called, a symbol of the spear in its leaf; and of the five wounds in its five anthers. The tendrils were likened to the cords and whips, and the column of the ovary to the pillar of the Cross. The stamens symbolized the hammers, and the dark circle of threads the crown of thorns. Thus the Maracoc became known as the Passion flower and its symbol, Religious Fervour.

Pink   *Perfection*

Pinks have been bred in many forms and colours, each with a different meaning in the Language of Flowers, and 'as pretty as a pink', still remains as neat a compliment to a young girl as she could wish. But if one sentiment can stand for all, surely 'the pink of perfection' will do?

Poppy   *Sleep, dreams and fantasy*

All poppies are narcotic, but it is the white poppy, with a purple stain at the base of each petal, *Papaver somniferum*, which should have as its sentiment the Sleep and the Dreams and the Fantasy that it brings.

Too shy to obey the instructions on this charming card, the sender has simply written *Nacissus* on the reverse side. We can only hope that the reply was not a *white rose* sent by special delivery.

Primrose   *Early youth*

A New Year has begun before the first primrose appears, yet at its appearance the year is still young enough to bring us hope.

Rosemary   *Remembrance*

Shakespeare did not invent the Language of Flowers, which was compiled long after his death, but small scraps of flower lore can be found in many of his plays. That he already knew of the meaning of this much-loved plant may be heard in Ophelia's plaintive offer to Laertes, her brother, 'There's rosemary, that's for remembrance, pray, love, remember.'

Rose   *Silence*

This sentiment refers to the custom in ancient Rome in which at feasts and festivals a rose upon the ceiling was an indication that nothing which passed beneath it should be revealed. The rose being sacred to Silence, not one word spoken 'under the rose' was ever repeated.

[107]

Rue *Repentance*

Known as the Herb of Grace from its use at High Mass on Sunday, it was also called the Herb of Repentance, and was once eaten to avoid talking in one's sleep. A useful herb for husbands, and for wives too, for that matter, for after talking in one's sleep, Repentance may well follow.

Saffron *Marriage*

The origin of the symbolism of Marriage for this plant probably lies in ancient Greece and Rome, when it was said of brides to be that 'They shall wear the bridal saffron', and the wedding bed was decorated with its flowers.

Snowdrop *Consolation*

In the almost total absence of other flowers, the chill-veined Fair Maid of February as she is called, is indeed a consolation to the house-bound gardener.

Star of Bethlehem *Reconciliation*

The Star of Bethlehem, symbol of the Reconciliation between God and man, was used by the Victorians in the Language of Flowers as a flower of reconciliation between man and woman.

Strawberry *Perfection*

It may have been Isaak Walton's quotation of Dr Botelier's description of the strawberry, 'Doubtless God could have made a better berry, but doubtless God never did', which has made it the emblem of Perfection, and doubtless one cannot deny it.

Tulip *A Declaration of love*

Although it is universally accepted that a Turkish lover declared his love by proffering a red tulip to his lady, this has never been regarded as the English lover's way. The tulip may be the artist's flower or the gardener's flower, but it can never take the place of the red rose where British emotions are concerned, and we have Robbie Burns and Interflora to prove it.

Vine *Mirth*

In including the vine and its sentiment in his Language of Flowers, Arthur Freeling hastened to add, 'We willingly acknowledge it, then; as the emblem of Mirth, being assured that our fair friends, at any rate, will never take of the intoxicating qualities of its juice, and therefor only know it by the health and good humour its moderate use imparts.' Mirth for men only.

Violet *Faithfulness*

In *A Nosegay always sweet, for lovers to send for tokens of love at New Year's Tide, or for fairings*, believed to be by William Hunnis, who died in 1597, we find either the source, or at least confirmation of this emblem.

> Violet is for faithfulness
>   Which in me shall abide;
> Hoping likewise that from your heart
>   You will not let it slide;
> And will continue in the same
>   As you have now begun,
> And then for ever to abide,
>   Then you my heart have won.

Wallflower *Fidelity in misfortune*

The sentiment of the wallflower dates back to the troubadours of the twelfth century, for it is known that they carried a sprig of wallflower as an avowal that their love would survive time and misfortune. Their belief in this plant was based on the fact that it was and still is found growing on ruins and fallen towers, shedding its fragrance while surrounded by desolation.

Weeping willow *Forsaken*

No one since has seemed to enjoy their own sorrow more than lovers who, forsaken by their loved one, or deprived by death, were said to 'wear the willow'.

> In love, the sad forsaken wight
> The willow garland weareth.

> Anon.

Bibliography

Anon., *The Imperial Royal Fortune Teller*, London, n.d.

Baker, Richard St Barbe, *Famous Trees of Bible Lands*, London, 1974.

Barrett, W. A., *Flowers and Festivals*, London, 1868.

Brand, John, *Popular Antiquities*, London, 1813.

Brewer, E. Cobham, *Dictionary of Phrase and Fable*, London, 1901.

Bulfinch, Thomas, *The Age of Fable*, London, 1969.

Crowfoot, G. M. and Baldensperger, L., *From Cedar to Hyssop*, London, 1932.

Culpeper, Nicholas, *Complete Herbal*, Manchester, 1826.

Dowling, Alfred E. P. R., *The Flora of the Sacred Nativity*, London, 1900.

Folkard, Richard, *Plant Lore, Legends and Lyrics*, London, 1884.

Frazer, Sir J. G., *The Golden Bough*, London, 1925.

Freeling, Arthur, *Flowers, Their Use and Beauty*, London, 1857.

Friend, Hilderic, *Flowers and Flower Lore*, London, 1884.

Grieve, M., *A Modern Herbal*, London, 1976.

Grigson, Geoffrey, *The Englishman's Flora*, London, 1960.

Hazlitt, W. Carew, *Gleanings in Old Garden Literature*, London, 1887.

Hole, Christina, *Witchcraft in England*, London, 1977.

Kennedy-Bell, M. G., *The Glory of the Garden*, London, 1923.

Larwood, J. and Hotten, J. C., *The History of Signboards*, London, 1875.

Lehner, Ernst and Johanna, *Folklore and Symbolism of Flowers, Plants and Trees*, USA, 1960.

Lemprière, J., *Classical Dictionary*, London, 1831.

Leyel, Mrs C. F., *The Magic of Herbs*, London, 1932.

Loudon, J. C., *Encyclopædia of Trees and Shrubs*, London, 1869.

Maundeville or Manderville, Sir John, *The Voiage and Travaile of Sir John Maundeville*, 14th century. English version 15th century.

Parkins, Dr, *The English Physician*, London, 1826.

Parkinson, John, *Paradisi in Sole Paradisus in Terristris*, London, 1629.

Phillips, Henry, *Sylva Florifera*, London, 1823.

Philpot, Mrs J. H., *The Sacred Tree*, London, 1897.

Pratt, Anne, *Flowering Plants of Great Britain*, London, 1870.

Rohde, Eleanour Sinclair, *The Old English Herbals*, London, 1972.

Standish, Robert, *The First of Trees*, London, 1960.

Taylor, Gladys, *Saints and Their Flowers*, London, 1956.

Thistleton-Dyer, T. F., *The Folklore of Plants*, London, 1889.

Tyas, Robert, *The Language of Flowers*, London, 1869.

Walker, Winifred, *All the Plants of the Bible*, London, 1959.

Woodforde, James, *The Diary of a Country Parson*, 1758–1802, Oxford, 1979.

Index